Patricia Bosworth's books include critically acclaimed biographies of Diane Arbus and Montgomery Clift and a memoir, *Anything Your Little Heart Desires*. She is a contributing editor to *Vanity Fair* and writes regularly for the *New York Times* and *Mirabella*. She lives in New York City.

MARLON
BRANDO

PATRICIA
BOSWORTH

PHOENIX

A PHOENIX PAPERBACK

First published in Great Britain in 2001
By Weidenfeld & Nicolson
This paperback edition published in 2002
by Phoenix,
an imprint of Orion Books Ltd,
Orion House, 5 Upper St Martin's Lane,
London WC2H 9EA

First published in USA in 2001
by Viking/Penguin

A CIP catalogue record for this book
is available from the British Library.

ISBN 0 75381 379 3

Printed and bound in Great Britain by
Clays Ltd, St Ives plc

For my husband, Tom Palumbo

ILLUSTRATIONS

Acting is half shame, half glory.
Shame at exhibiting yourself
—glory when you can forget yourself.

—John Gielgud

In 1952 photographer Ruth Orkin captured Brando engrossed in a chess game on the set of the film *Julius Caesar*. There is such simplicity and balance in this image, because it totally contains his silence.

1

MARLON BRANDO, NICKNAMED BUD, was born on April 3, 1924, in Omaha, Nebraska. At the time much of the state was recovering from a grasshopper plague that had turned the sky green. Enormous humming clouds ate all the crops and left the fields and gardens brown and bare.

Brando was the only son of Dorothy ("Dodie") Pennebaker, a radiant, unconventional blonde of Irish heritage, and Marlon Brando, Sr., a salesman for Western Limestone products, who'd inherited a violent temper and martinet ways from his father, Eugene Brandeaux, of French Alsatian extraction. Senior changed his name to Brando shortly before he married Dodie on June 22, 1918. They had had a passionate courtship, starting in high school, and had written many love letters to each other when Senior was serving in the Army during World War I. Brando saved some of the letters but maintained that they did not move him.

Brando lived with his parents and his two older sisters, Jocelyn and Frances, in a comfortable wood-frame house at 3135 Mason. They were frequently visited by "Nana," their twice-married, independent-minded grandmother, who was known for her outspoken views on immigration and women's rights and as a master speed reader. Nana was also a devout Christian Scientist and a lay healer; in later years she would say she could speak with the dead. Often Nana spent hours with her daughter Dodie and her grandchildren, discussing history, religion, art, politics. "She inspired us," Jocelyn remembers, and Brando and his sisters needed inspiration.

Their father, Marlon Senior, was a moody, unpredictable man given to fierce rages, and they were terrified of him, although he was rarely with his family. He spent most of his time traveling all over Missouri and Iowa as a salesman. He was often seen in Chicago brothels and speakeasies; he had frequent affairs. When he returned home, he and Dodie would drink heavily and fight. It was Prohibition, so they brewed their beer in the kitchen.

In 1926, when Brando was two, he and his family moved with Nana to a bigger house at 1026 Third Street, and Dodie began filling the living room with bohemians and oddballs, as well as friends from the community theater, such as the Fonda family and the parents of Dorothy McGuire, the actress.

The atmosphere was relaxed and casual. Dodie often received people in bed, her quilt littered with magazines and crossword puzzles. Brando has told friends that his earliest memory was lying in bed with his mother, sharing a bowl of milk and crackers.

Although Dodie truly loved her children, she was seldom home. Housework bored her, and she was hopelessly stage-struck. Just before Brando was born, she'd joined the fledgling

Omaha Community Playhouse, and she escaped there whenever she could, even attending rehearsals of shows she had no part in. She sat in on auditions and gave the young Henry Fonda his first job. Over the next four years she played many roles, from Eugene O'Neill's Anna Christie to Julie in Ferenc Molnár's *Liliom*. The local critic said of that performance: "Mrs. Brando is profoundly moving (especially in the death scene). Her reserve has the effect of numbing in sorrow," and another wrote, "Amazingly realistic."

With his mother away from the house so much, Brando began relying on the loving attention of his nurse, Ermeline, who was "Danish, but a touch of Indonesian blood gave her skin a slightly dark, smoky patina," as he writes in his autobiography. At night they would sleep together in the nude, and Brando, then age five, would wake up and look down at her body and fondle her breasts, and then he would crawl all over her. "She was all mine; she belonged to me and to me alone."

When he was seven, Ermi left him to get married, and Brando felt abandoned. He began to stutter. He was a fat-bellied little boy, serious and determined, with a penetrating stare and boundless energy. Jocelyn had to take him to kindergarten on a leash; otherwise he would have run away.

In 1930 Senior got a better job in Illinois as the general manager for the Calcium Carbonate Company, so the family moved to Evanston. Dodie agreed to the move, but she resented it; she had to leave the playhouse at the height of her success. Her drinking increased. She would say, "I'm the greatest actress *not* on the American stage." Senior was always away. Sometimes she would wander around their new house on Sheridan Square, crying. Then she would sit down at the piano and begin singing. Her children would sing with her.

"My mother knew every song that was ever written," Brando writes in his autobiography. He memorized as many of them as he could. Today he can still remember the lyrics of all those songs: Greek songs, Japanese songs, Irish songs, German songs, American songs—all the songs his mother ever taught him.

By the time he was eight, Bud Brando was the "star" of the neighborhood, mimicking people, climbing in and out of windows (something he would do for much of his life), swinging at the end of a rope while letting loose with a Johnny Weissmuller yell so piercing it could be heard for blocks. He was "a free spirit," a friend remembers, "a real individualist. Even as a little kid you knew he was going to do anything he set out to do. And he was a prankster. Like he'd pull the fire alarm and then race off and hide when the fire engines zoomed down the street."

At Lincoln School he was very popular. He and another sixth grader, Wally Cox—frail, bespectacled, and skinny—became inseparable. "Marlon thought Wally was a genius. Maybe he was," said Pat Cox, Wally's third wife. "He certainly was tremendously knowledgeable, an omnivorous reader. Even at the age of ten he knew about botany, the names of different butterflies and birds, and every wildflower in the world. He and Marlon would hike all over the place, talking a mile a minute." They loved to have contests: Who can eat faster? Who can hold his breath longer?

Wally's mother was a mystery writer. She also was an alcoholic, so Wally and his sister were often left to be cared for by

Brando at the age of eight with his beloved mother, Dodie, probably the most important person in his life.

near strangers whenever Mrs. Cox went off on a binge. Later she abandoned them for a lesbian lover. Soon Wally was dropping by the Brando house; he would stay for supper and then the night. "Wally became like a member of the family," Jocelyn says, and when he was tormented by classmates, Brando would protect him as he protected sick animals and bums. He once brought a bag lady home from off the street. She was in rags and seemed quite ill. Brando had a tantrum until Senior agreed to take the bag lady to a nearby hotel where she could recuperate in a clean bed.

By 1936 Senior's philandering had become so extreme that Dodie was beside herself. One night when he came home with lipstick smeared on his underpants, she started screaming and crying, and he took her into their bedroom and began beating her. Brando, age twelve, rushed into the bedroom and threatened to kill his father if he didn't stop. It was a scene that Brando later described to his friends over and over, and he would refer to his father's unpredictable nature: affectionate and sensitive one minute and livid with anger the next.

He was repelled by what he felt was his father's hypocrisy. Although Senior was raising his kids by the "Good Book," he was a relentless womanizer, and by forcing the family to move from Omaha, he'd ruined Dodie's life by depriving her of her career on the stage; he had no compassion for her huge despair.

Throughout his adolescence rage propelled Brando: rage against his father and fantasies of revenge. Decades later, in the 1980s, with the help of his therapist he would realize how his family had been an incubator of psychological violence, and that society had no way of controlling it or of stopping it because it was a private family matter, conducted behind closed doors.

For a while Dodie and the children went to California to live with her half sister, Betty Lindemeyer, and Nana. Brando and his sisters attended Lathrop Junior High School. A couple of times Henry Fonda visited and drove Dodie to Hollywood; he had never forgotten how she had given him his start. But she was drinking a lot and sometimes disappeared for days at a time.

Two years later, in 1938, the Brandos reconciled, and Senior bought an old farmhouse in Libertyville, Illinois, thirty-five miles outside Chicago. There was a barn and stables and acres of land. Brando loved the animals "because an animal's love is unconditional." He especially loved his dog, Dutchy, a Great Dane, and a cow named Violet. "I'd ride Violet out into the field and I'd put my arms around her and kiss her. Cows have very sweet breath because of the hay they eat."

But life was no better for Brando on the farm. Dodie hated housework and hated being so isolated in the country, and the place was often a mess. Brando was doing poorly in school. He'd stay in his room, listening to Gene Krupa records. He loved playing the drums, and he carried his drumsticks everywhere, beating out a frantic tat-tat on coffee tables and desktops. He drummed so much he'd forget to milk the cows or do his homework, and then his father would get after him, and they'd start yelling at each other on the porch. Dodie would say, "Can't you have a civilized discussion? Why can't you speak normally?" and she'd shoo them out into the backyard, where they'd continue to shout. Often Brando would simply run off.

He was starting to date. One of his first girlfriends, Carmelita Pope, remembers inviting him over for pasta; after they'd eaten, he would go out on the sunporch with her father, who was a lawyer, and ask him all sorts of questions. Brando was insatiably curious about everything. He was quite fat then, and Senior insisted he work out with barbells and bench presses until he transformed himself into the body beautiful.

He kept on playing the drums and founded a band called Keg Brando and His Kegliners. But his grades got worse. At school he excelled only in sports and in dramatics, especially pantomime. He failed all his other subjects and was held back a year. He was close to sixteen and still a sophomore. It was humiliating; he became a truant.

When his father found out, there were more violent shouting matches. Brando did not remind him that often instead of attending classes he went to Chicago to hunt for his mother, whom he usually found slumped in some bar passed out in her own vomit. One time he dragged her naked into a cab and brought her home; again Senior started to beat her, and again Brando managed to stop him.

In May 1941 Brando was expelled from Libertyville High for chronic misbehavior. His last prank had been pouring hydrosulfate into the blower at school so a rotten-egg smell pervaded the classrooms. He possessed a love of mischief other students found admirable.

Senior was hopping mad. After much deliberation he packed his son off to his alma mater, Shattuck Military Academy in Fairbault, Minnesota, where he had been an honor student. The same would not hold true for Brando; he had poor study habits, and his concentration span was short. He simply could not conform. He was sixteen then, startlingly handsome, with a Roman nose and a sensual mouth, and his taut, muscled body practically undulated when he moved, like a graceful tomcat on the prowl.

He was funny; he had no pretenses. He refused to kowtow to the school bullies, and he acted tough, often insolent. He would fight anyone who came on to him; he had a hair-trigger temper. He loved challenging authority and could not be controlled. Once he wrote "shit" on the blackboard and then lit a fuse doused in Vitalis, which contained alcohol, and *poof!* the word became indelible on the board. Another time he stole all the silver from the dining room so the cadets couldn't eat their breakfast; classes were delayed until the silver was found. The student body thought his pranks were audacious; he became very popular. (Brando says his favorite prank was his disabling of the school's bell. The noise so maddened him that one night he shimmied up to the bell tower and cut the clapper off, then buried it.)

He writes, "I had a great deal of satisfaction challenging authority successfully. I had no sense of emotional security. I didn't know later why I felt valueless or that I responded to worthlessness with hostility."

He has said he was encouraged by only one teacher, Duke Wagner, who taught him Shakespeare and the glory of language and who perceived his great natural gift for mimicry. Once Brando transformed himself into the gangster John Dillinger and had all the students squirming in their seats. On Thanksgiving in 1941 he performed in three one-act plays at Shattuck. The school newspaper wrote, "The new boy shows enormous talent."

However, his grades continued to be poor. Every week he wrote to his parents, asking them to believe in him and telling them over and over how much he loved them, hoping his words would persuade them to say they loved him. But Senior and Dodie never wrote him back or visited him in the two years he was at Shattuck.

The summer of 1942 Brando did not go home to Libertyville right away. Instead he rode the rails and lived in hobo camps, sitting by campfires with the drifters, eating mulligan stew, listening to their stories, how some were hiding out from police or irate wives. He learned their lingo and their sign language; a certain sign marked in chalk on a fence meant the neighbor down the road was hospitable.

Back on the farm, he and his mother had a disjointed conversation about his going into the theater later on when he'd finished high school. But he was thinking he might become a minister, he writes in his autobiography, "Not because I was a religious person, other than having an inexhaustible awe and reverence for nature, but because I thought it might give me more of a purpose in life." Actually he had no idea what he wanted to do.

Returning to Shattuck, he dyed his hair red. He made twelve visits to the infirmary (he faked a fever by holding the thermometer to a hot-water bottle). He was the school's reigning clown and rebel, loved and admired by everybody. That fall he won the lead role in *Four on a Heath* and was able to show off his remarkable ability to take on an accent (in this case, English). In the final scene of the play he hanged himself and did it so realistically that, after the curtain came down, the audience burst into frenzied applause and his performance was the talk of the school.

But he continued to flunk all his courses. He'd hide out in the study hall, reading *National Geographic*. One afternoon he came across some color photographs of the island of Tahiti, with its pure white sands and thick, rustling palms. And the expression on the Polynesian natives' faces—it was an expression he'd never seen: "happy, unmanaged faces," he wrote, open maps of contentment. He vowed he would go to Tahiti someday.

In May 1943 Brando was put on probation at Shattuck for talking back to an officer during maneuvers. It was considered insubordination, so he was confined to campus. But after a couple of hours he got bored and took off for downtown Fairbault. Of course, his absence was discovered. When he returned to the school, hours later, he was sent to his room, and the faculty met to decide his fate. He was promptly expelled.

Brando recalls that it was a shock. He wandered from room to room in a daze, saying good-bye to all his friends. When he reached Duke Wagner's office, the teacher reassured him that everything would be all right and that the world would hear from him someday. Brando has said that he will never forget those words; no one had ever expressed confidence in him before. Then Wagner hugged him tightly, and Brando found himself sobbing uncontrollably in the teacher's arms.

He took the train home almost immediately. His parents seemed bitterly disappointed in him.

Meanwhile, at Shattuck, the entire student body was up in

arms about his expulsion, feeling it was both extreme and unfair. Eventually the students went on strike and stayed on strike until the faculty agreed that he be reinstated. The principal then wrote to Brando, inviting him to complete his studies and be graduated the following year. But he hated the military academy so much he refused to go back. He never graduated from high school, but for years he kept the cadets' letter of support framed in the bedroom of his home in Beverly Hills. He has always felt embarrassed by his lack of education.

For the next six weeks after leaving Shattuck, Brando dug ditches for the Tile Drainage Company. His father had arranged the job for him, and he loathed every minute of it, although he did enjoy earning money on his own. But home life on the farm was lonely. His sister Frances was in New York, trying to be a painter, and Jocelyn was there too; she'd already appeared in one Broadway play. By fall Brando had decided to join them. He'd visited Frannie in New York briefly the previous Christmas and had written her afterward that he wanted to live there.

He might even try acting, he thought. His father's response was to scoff, "The theater? That's for faggots! It's not man's work." Then he added that Brando could never be a success anyway: "Take a look in the mirror and tell me if anyone would want to see a yokel like you on the stage!" Hearing the contempt in Senior's voice, knowing he had no faith in him, made Brando want all the more to excel at *something* to prove himself. But at what?

2

HE ARRIVED IN NEW YORK during the late spring of 1943, dressed in faded dungarees and sporting a red fedora. "I thought I was going to knock everybody dead," he says. The first thing he did was to have his shoes shined in the midst of the bustle of Penn Station. He felt sorry for the little shoeshine boy and tipped him five dollars. Then he grabbed his duffel bag and plunged into the crowds surging on West Thirty-fourth Street.

After living on a farm and in small towns all his life, he was astonished by the noise, heat, dust, and confusion of wartime New York. He couldn't get over the honking, gridlocked traffic, the welter of neon signs at Times Square. And so many people! Refugees from Hitler's Germany, artists, musicians, poets, everybody cramming into New York, hoping to find fame and fortune.

He kept bumping into servicemen on leave, all out for a good time. Brando had smashed a knee during football practice at Shattuck, and he had poor eyesight, so he was 4-F, a fact that didn't bother him. He had no interest in going off to battle, but his father was disappointed.

For a while Brando roomed with his sister Frannie, who lived in a tiny apartment on Patchin Place. He was hardly ever there; he stayed up all night, went to parties, observed everybody very seriously. "He was naïve," his sister Jocelyn recalled. "It took him awhile to become disillusioned with people. He was so trusting."

Brando's first serious girlfriend was Celia Webb, an intense, elegant little lady from South America. She was ten years older than he, with a young son. She lived across the hall from Frannie in a one-room apartment. Her husband was away in the Army.

Celia was a window dresser "and a great cook," someone said. Brando moved in with her, and they were together off and on for a long time. Their friendship lasted for many years. "She was very important to me, but after [Celia] there were many other women," he says.

"Marlon controlled his women," says the dancer Sondra Lee, who was another one of Brando's early girlfriends. "It was never a situation of equals." She recalls dropping by to visit him in a fleabag hotel, one of many he inhabited before he became a movie star. "Marlon opened the door, and behind him there was Celia in bed. Marlon was very charming to me, but I got the message I couldn't stay. We all knew she was special." Sondra became friends with Celia. "In those days all of Marlon's girls were friends. We accepted the situation with him. He was like a god, a king. We accepted the fact he was different. It was rather unsettling. He seemed to have appeared out of nowhere, as if he were from another world. He would never allow himself to be tied down."

As soon as Brando's money ran out, he got a job as an elevator operator at Best's department store. He was also a short-order cook and a night watchman in a factory. After work he'd regale his sisters with silent portraits of the people he'd been observing on the subway: the gum-chewing secretary adjusting her stockings; the one-legged derelict begging for pennies outside Carnegie Hall. Brando could transform himself into anybody instantly, and the transformation was completely organic. "If he played an electrician, you could see the wires," someone said.

Friends encouraged him to become an actor. Why not? He had great natural gifts and was trained for no other profession. But he still wasn't sure that was what he really wanted to do. Maybe he'd become a writer or a director. The one thing he really wanted was to be educated. The next time his father phoned from Libertyville, Brando said, "Pop, I'm going to study at the New School." Senior agreed to send him tuition money but added that he hadn't much hope, he wasn't going to amount to anything. That made Brando want to try harder, to prove his father wrong.

In the fall of 1943 Brando enrolled in the Dramatic Workshop of the New School for Social Research, on Twelfth Street in Greenwich Village. The workshop had been established in 1940 and was a magnet for aspiring actors from all over the country. In Brando's class were Harry Belafonte, Elaine Stritch, Gene Saks, Shelley Winters, Rod Steiger, and Kim Stanley, to name only a few.

Brando took fencing, dance, and yoga and studied with the dictatorial German émigré Erwin Piscator, a small, highly keyed man who'd revolutionized European theater by using bare stages and harsh, realistic lighting. Brando resisted Piscator's authoritarian ways, much preferring the classes he took with the master acting teacher Stella Adler, the flamboyant, imperious former member of the Yiddish theater and the daughter of the great Yiddish actor Jacob Adler.

Mercurial, with thick blond hair, huge, expressive blue eyes, and a curly mouth, Adler exuded a glamour and a kind of radiant intelligence Brando had never seen before. Her teaching was volatile and scholarly; her lectures, especially on Chekhov and Ibsen, were delivered with a passionate evangelism. She kept her students spellbound, alternately raging and purring as she spoke. She dared them to use their imaginations, to be larger than themselves, and, above all, *never to be boring.*

Adler's most creative years had been spent in the 1930s with the Group Theatre, the experimental Depression-era company founded by Harold Clurman, Lee Strasberg, and Cheryl Crawford. It was a pivotal moment in the growth of American theater, uniting playwrights such as Clifford Odets and William Saroyan, directors like Elia Kazan, and actors such as John Garfield and Franchot Tone, who worked to shape theater that was often politically relevant. Members of the ensemble were leading interpreters of the Method, and the Method revolutionized American theater. In the past, classical acting instruction had focused on developing external talents, while Method acting was the first systematized training that developed internal abilities—sensory, psychological, and emotional.

Strasberg, who later headed the Actors Studio, rooted his

view of the Method in what Konstantin Stanislavsky had stressed early in his career: that the actor should perform affective memory exercises, improvise, and conjure up the conscious past to convey emotion—for example, dwell on personal tragedy to show anguish.

Adler opposed this approach. In 1934 she went to Paris with Harold Clurman, and she studied with Stanislavsky for five weeks. She found he'd revised his theories. He now stressed that the actor should create by imagination rather than memory, and that the key to success was "the truth. Truth in the circumstances of the play."

Adler's precepts for acting revolved around concentration, attention to detail, and the creation of specific physical action for the character. "Your truth is in your imagination," she said. "The rest is lice." She believed that the art, architecture, and clothes of an era were crucial to shaping a role, and she always explored texts for performance clues. However, in class, she didn't work with plays that much; instead she used improvisations and exercises to release the actors' inhibitions. "Don't act. Behave," was one of her mottoes.

All her New School students were neatly dressed, so when Brando appeared in her class wearing threadbare dungarees and filthy sneakers, she did an exaggerated double take. "Who's the vagabond?" she demanded.

"Marlon Brando," he answered, staring at her until she blushed. His handsome, sullen face was stubbly with beard.

Within weeks she was calling him "extraordinary." It was probably because of what he achieved so effortlessly in the first animal exercise she gave him. She'd instructed the entire class to behave like chickens in a henhouse after they were told that a bomb was about to explode over them. While the other students hopped frantically around the room, clucking and flapping their arms like wings, Brando sat quietly in a corner miming the laying of an egg. "That's exactly what a chicken would do under the circumstances, my darling!" Adler exclaimed.

He was nineteen when they met. She was forty-one and "very beautiful," Brando recalls. Soon she was inviting him to her overdone apartment on West Fifty-fourth Street and introducing him to her four sisters; her daughter, Ellen; her eighty-year-old mother, Sarah; and her second husband, the esteemed critic and former Group Theatre director Harold Clurman. Sometimes Brando accompanied them to a Childs restaurant on Columbus Circle, where they had coffee and bagels with the playwright Clifford Odets.

Other times he sat in her living room, mimicking her every move. She'd sip scotch, he'd sip scotch; she'd light a cigarette, he'd light a cigarette; she'd cross her legs and finally notice what he was doing and say, "Oh, Marlon, stop it!" She found his ability to take on the physical characteristics of other people truly remarkable. Later she said, "he takes in everything, including the size of your teeth." Brando eventually took in her vanity and willfulness and used it in a variety of characters over the years. He had no fear of his androgeny. He loved playing around with gender.

Adler had appeared in more than a hundred plays; she'd been acting since childhood. She was a bravura actress who'd never been given the chance to be a huge star in Hollywood, as she longed to be. She wanted to be recognized and famous. She was bitterly disappointed that she wasn't.

"Stella taught me everything," he would say. She would say, "I taught Marlon nothing. I only opened the doors to feeling and experience, and he walked right through them, and after that he didn't need me." Philip Rhodes, Brando's close friend and makeup man for forty years, says, "Stella showed Marlon how to focus his anger towards his father; she helped him channel it creatively."

By December, Brando was appearing in Dramatic Workshop shows. His first appearance was in G. B. Shaw's *Saint Joan*. He followed that with J. M. Synge's *Riders to the Sea*, and then he played Prince Anatole in Piscator's condensed version of Tolstoy's *War and Peace*. "He was always ready, like Mozart," said a fellow student. "Everybody else was struggling, but for Marlon there was no sign of struggle or effort."

Then in January 1944 Brando played the double role of the young Jesus Christ and a doddering old schoolteacher in Gerhart Hauptmann's *Hannele's Way to Heaven*. "Marlon was absolutely breathtaking," says Elaine Stritch. "You knew you were in the presence of an acting genius." He followed that tour de force with roles in Shakespeare, Moliére, and a children's play by Stanley Kauffmann titled *Bobino,* in which he performed "a brilliant little pantomime."

By then he'd reunited with Wally Cox, his dear childhood friend from Evanston. Cox, still skinny and bespectacled, was working as a silversmith and puppeteer to help support his mother, who was suffering from a partial paralysis.

He and Brando sat for hours, talking about sex and death and love and women. Everett Greenbaum, who later wrote *Mr. Peepers* for Cox, says, "What bonded them was their intense curiosity about everything in the universe. Wally spoke four languages and knew about insects, botany, and birds. He understood every page in *Scientific American*." But both men were "also attracted to the dark side."

"Marlon especially, he really went for trash, for creeps—both men and women," says another friend. "Rita Moreno was one of the few decent women he ever went with. Marlon dug the worst aspects of life, and of himself, and then he used them for himself as an actor and turned them around—like years later, in *The Godfather*, where you see this evil criminal playing so lovingly with his grandson."

Meanwhile, life on the farm in Libertyville had become unbearable for Dodie. Senior had joined AA and wanted her to do the same, but she could not give up drinking. So she left him and went to New York—to be with her children, she said. After arriving in April 1944, with the family's ancient Great Dane, Dutchy, in tow, she rented a drafty ten-room apartment on West End Avenue. Senior had agreed to pay for everything, including a part-time maid.

Jocelyn moved in, with her new baby son and husband, the actor Don Hanmer, who was on leave from the Army. Frannie and Brando remained in the Village, although Brando dropped by as often as he could, and an assortment of friends usually tagged along with him. The apartment filled up with artists and writers, singers and dancers. The place was never empty.

Dodie would hold court from her bed, and Brando would visit her there. Sometimes he attempted to shock her: He would put on her frilly bathrobe and vamp around in it, especially if he had an audience. He would tease and badger her, and she seemed to enjoy it. Sometimes he tried to provoke her. Once, when they both were in the kitchen, Brando peed in the sink. "Oh, Buddy," his mother cried to others in the room, "why doesn't he stop this shit?"

Everyone who saw them together was aware of their deep emotional bond. "Bud worshiped and adored Dodie," Elaine Stritch said. Dodie in turn idolized him. He was her genius. Somehow she believed that part of that genius was in her too, that he'd inherited it from her.

He was worried about her. The apartment was a mess: dirty dishes in the sink, meals served haphazardly, if at all. She was in the last agonies of alcoholism. She stashed liquor all over the apartment, and he and his sisters could never find it.

Soon Dodie was disappearing for days, and Brando would prowl around every bar on the West Side, hoping to find her. When he couldn't, he would come back to her apartment and sink into a depression. His feelings of abandonment and resentment and fear would all merge, and then he would have to go to class and perform. Eventually he and his sisters began accompanying Dodie to AA meetings.

That summer Brando joined Piscator's little theater group out in Sayville, Long Island, where he repeated his triumph in the *Hannele* play. He had such charisma that the audience gasped when he made his first entrance, in a gold satin suit. One night MCA's powerful theatrical agent Maynard Morris caught the show, and afterward he went backstage and told Brando he wanted to represent him. Brando appeared indifferent.

He was more interested in girls. He juggled many girls that

summer: Celia Webb; a singer, Janice Mars; and a voluptuous young blonde named Blossom Plumb. Near midsummer Piscator caught him holding hands with Blossom in the barn and expelled them from the company immediately, although they both heatedly denied they were doing anything wrong. Later Piscator regretted his action and admitted that Marlon Brando was the most gifted actor he had ever taught, although he wished "he hadn't been so lazy."

In the fall Morris and his colleague at MCA, Edie Van Cleve, started sending Brando out on auditions. He soon got a part in John Van Druten's Broadway play *I Remember Mama*, playing the role of Nels, a fifteen-year-old Norwegian-American who wants to become a doctor and has an eloquent coming-of-age speech in the third act. Stella Adler read the script and predicted it would be a hit. She urged Brando to do it.

During rehearsals he mumbled so much that Richard Rodgers, who was producing the show, wanted him fired. But Van Druten, who was also directing, said no. He could see that even though Brando was inexperienced, he had so much presence he was already upstaging the leads, veteran actors Mady Christians and Oscar Homolka.

Before the show opened on October 19, 1944, Brando handed his bio, scrawled on a piece of paper, to the play's press agent. It read, "Born in Calcutta, India, where his father was engaged in geological research, he came to this country when he was six months old." It was published in the *Playbill* program as written, much to Senior's exasperation when he was shown the program later.

On opening night Dodie was suffering from such a terrible

hangover she didn't see her only son make his Broadway debut, a huge disappointment to them both. His sisters and some friends attended, as did the director Robert Lewis, who later taught Brando at the Actors Studio. He remembers seeing "this young boy wander downstage munching an apple. He was so natural I thought he really did live upstairs. He just stood there and said nothing for two minutes, but the way he *listened,* you could not take your eyes off him. He didn't seem to be acting. He was also completely relaxed."

After the curtain came down, friends joined him for a party at Dodie's West End Avenue apartment to celebrate. A few of his women were there, and the scruffy types he had been collecting, such as Carlo Fiore, a would-be actor who kept trying to kick his heroin habit. Brando ignored everybody and headed straight to his mother's bedroom. He found Dodie propped up on the pillows, confiding to one of his friends that she'd better go back to Chicago because she was causing her kids too much trouble with her drinking. But she didn't leave New York until the middle of the following year.

I Remember Mama was a big hit, and Brando remained with the show for the duration of its run. The demands of the part weren't that great, so he brought stacks of books back to his dressing room—philosophy, religion, the plays of Shakespeare and O'Neill—and he read them from cover to cover. He also kept tabs on his mother; he watched her relentlessly. They both knew she couldn't go on drinking so much.

Dodie had to have help; she could not stop drinking on her own. Then she met a smart, tough woman from AA named Marty Mann, who'd been the first woman to acknowledge publicly that she was an alcoholic at an AA meeting, and who eventually did studies at Yale proving that alcoholism is a disease. Dodie was impressed by her. She went with her to meetings, and with her encouragement and support, she decided to commit herself totally to AA.

She told her son of her plan to return to Chicago to go into AA and to reconcile with Senior. Brando pleaded with her to remain in New York. He did not want her to go back to his father. But she was adamant. Dodie was really in love with Senior. She told Elaine Stritch that she was "mad about the bastard." As soon as his mother left him, Brando began stammering. He couldn't eat and lost twenty-five pounds. After the show he would wander the streets for hours, panicked, and he didn't know why. He felt that way for many months. He writes in his autobiography that he had "a kind of nervous breakdown," and although he recovered from it, he "never felt quite whole again."

Brando continues: "Stella Adler's family...virtually adopted me after my mother left, and they may have saved my sanity." He used to go into Adler's bedroom when she was getting ready for dinner. She'd be sitting in her bra and panties, and she'd cover herself up. "Oh, Marlon. Please, darling. I'm getting dressed." And he'd say, "That's why I'm here, in order to see that you're dressed *properly*." A couple of times he grabbed her breasts in his palms, "and she would say with a half smile, 'Marlon, don't do that or I'll slap you.'

"I would look at her and say, 'You know you don't want to do that to me.'"

The two of them had a lot of flirtatious exchanges, and "there was the possibility of a real encounter, but it never materialized," he writes. "Stella gave me emotional strength at a time when I needed it," he goes on. "When I was suffering, disjointed and disoriented...she offered me not only her skill and talent as a teacher, but her home, her family, the largess of her personality and her love." He would sit next to her at noisy parties, and "she was forever holding my hand." She introduced him to the actors John Garfield and Franchot Tone, the conductor Leonard Bernstein, the playwrights Sidney Kingsley and William Saroyan.

Late at night, after the guests had gone, Brando would haltingly try to articulate his confusion about Dodie to Adler and Clurman, and the couple would listen sympathetically. Clurman later wrote, "Marlon suffers untold misery because of [his mother's] condition. The soul-searing pain of his childhood has lodged itself in some deep recess of his being. He hardly knows himself what it is.... But he has developed a mask, a front, that sometimes makes him lie, pretend, tease, play practical jokes." Clurman had already heard what Brando had done recently to Mady Christians onstage during a performance of *I Remember Mama*. He'd put salt in her coffee, and she'd vomited in the wings. He also did something to the doorknob on the set, so actors could not exit without pulling the knob off. He just had to find ways of alleviating the tedium of this long run. He drove the cast crazy with his tricks.

He also played the drums. He'd started taking a dance class at Katherine Dunham's, which featured exotic Afro-Caribbean dance styles and music, and he developed a passion for playing the congas. The drums brought Brando into contact with Haitians, Harlem blacks, and Latinos. Sometimes he pounded on the congas for hours, until the skin on his hands split. His drum teacher was Henri ("Papa")

Augustine, the company's *hungan,* or voodoo priest, who taught him that every rhythm had a purpose, such as healing or warding off evil spirits. Brando's passion for playing the congas has lasted his entire life.

Meanwhile Adler was convinced of his genius and kept trying to force him to overcome his seeming indifference to his talent and to the theater. She would talk to him about how creation is all that man has left; time goes, but what remains of Athens is the idea of beauty and the ruins of the Parthenon; only the artist is a revolutionary; artists can change the world—didn't he realize that?

3

IN FEBRUARY 1946 STELLA ADLER persuaded Harold Clurman to cast Brando in a play he was producing with the director Elia Kazan, his old colleague from the Group. It was a contemporary drama by Maxwell Anderson, titled *Truckline Cafe*, about a group of lost souls who congregate in a West Coast diner.

Brando was to play the part of Sage MacRae, a World War II vet who murders his unfaithful wife and throws her dead body into the sea (offstage), then confesses to the crime in a highly charged five-minute monologue.

It should be noted that Clurman and Kazan saw *Truckline Cafe* as one of the first postwar challenges to Broadway fluff, an assault on the status quo. Such New York playwrights of ideas as Anderson, Robert Sherwood (who'd written *Abe Lincoln in Illinois*), and the young Arthur Miller (who was soon to complete a play titled *All My Sons*, about a manufacturer who knowingly sells the U.S. government faulty airplane parts, resulting in the deaths of twenty-one pilots) were trying to reach out and touch a world changed irrevocably by the atomic bomb.

Kazan didn't really want Brando for *Truckline Cafe*. His audition had been lousy, but Clurman kept saying that the boy had real talent. They both agreed he had star quality. "It's like he's carrying his own spotlight," according to Kazan.

At that point Kazan was the hottest young director in America. His second movie, *A Tree Grows in Brooklyn*, had just opened to great acclaim, and earlier he'd directed Thornton Wilder's *Skin of Our Teeth* on Broadway. The play had won the Pulitzer Prize for drama.

Kazan was thirty-six, dark, stocky, driven, "with a devil's energy." He never stopped moving, never stopped taking notes. Originally he'd wanted to be a writer; later he became a novelist. He saw life as "both ridiculous and tragic at the same time—in that sense I'm an absurdist." A rug merchant's son from Turkey, he'd scrambled up from nothing to a scholarship at Williams and then at the Yale Drama School, before apprenticing at the Group as an actor. For a while he was Harold Clurman's stage manager. Indeed, the erudite, voluble Clurman, who was a couple of years older than Kazan, was his mentor. They argued about everything.

Like Brando, Kazan didn't talk very much. In fact, when they saw each other at the start of rehearsals in *Truckline*, they circled like animals, sizing each other up, then moving away without a word. Within a year Kazan proved to be the most significant force in Brando's career, but during those weeks, he was serving as producer, not director, of *Truckline*, so he just sat in the theater and watched rehearsals.

He decided very soon that he would someday work with

Brando. The guy was so instinctive, he thought. He *behaved* rather than acted. He internalized everything, picked up stuff like an X-ray.

Once or twice the two went off and played basketball on a court near Hell's Kitchen. Kazan had a thing about his body. He kept in tiptop shape by playing a lot of tennis and walking tirelessly around the city. Brando did the same; he exercised with weights too. It was nice to work up a sweat together. While they were playing basketball, they barely exchanged a word, and none about the play.

Major rewrites were needed with *Truckline*, and Kazan was worried about Clurman's sluggish direction. Midway through rehearsals some of the cast—actors Karl Malden and Kevin McCarthy—came to him and whispered he had to take over. All Harold was doing was talking about the play, they said, talking it to death.

The worst problem was Brando. He simply could not stop mumbling. Playwright Anderson wanted him fired, and so did his wife, but Clurman held off, believing there was a deep well of feeling in this young actor that he simply didn't know how to release. "He cannot voice the deepest part of himself; it hurts too much. That, in part, is the cause of his mumbling."

One afternoon the director ordered Brando to remain onstage and asked the others in the company to go back to their dressing rooms. Then Clurman ordered Brando to start shouting his lines, but the actor could barely get the words out. Clurman insisted, "Louder!" Brando was growing angry. Still, the lines seemed stuck in his throat. Clurman demanded, "Climb the rope!" and pointed to a thick rope hanging from the gridiron above the stage. Brando shimmied up like a monkey, as Clurman urged him to keep shouting out his lines.

Soon the rest of the cast ran from their dressing rooms to cluster in the wings, alarmed by Brando's frenzied cries. After he finished the speech, he dropped to the stage to face Clurman. He was panting and red-faced and "looked as if he were ready to hit me," Clurman recalled later. He told the young actor, "Now run the scene—normally," and he did, audibly and heartfelt. From then on he had no trouble, and on opening night his speech was rewarded with a thunderous ovation.

But it was Kazan who helped Brando achieve the stunning results in the "murder monologue" by telling him to run up and down the basement stairs of the theater until he was out of breath, just before he staggered on the stage to confess his crime. Then, seconds before he made his entrance, stage-hands doused him with a bucket of cold water so he burst out onstage soaking wet, trembling, and panting. Movie critic Pauline Kael, who saw him in the show, said, "That boy's having a convulsion! Then I realized he was acting."

Karl Malden, who watched the monologue from the wings, recalls that as Brando described shooting his wife six times, he hit the table in the diner six times for emphasis, with such force the table split in half. Audiences stomped and cheered when he finished the speech. Clurman maintained he hadn't seen such acting since John Barrymore. "It was terrific. It was inside him like an explosion."

That may have been, but the critics dismissed the show so savagely that Kazan and Clurman took out an ad lambasting their detractors and advising them to wise up. They pointed out that the radical fringe of 1930s theater was starting to move front and center; the public was longing for realistic, emotion-filled dramas, and the public knew what it wanted.

(This of course would be proved in the next decade. From 1944 to 1954, American drama came of age, with playwrights like the mature Eugene O'Neill, William Inge, Tennessee Williams, and Arthur Miller; their powerful works compensated for many years of superficial Broadway productions.)

Kazan and Clurman had hoped to sway public opinion with their ad, but it had no impact. The show closed after a week, but everyone was talking about "Marlon Brando, Marlon Brando." Kazan remarked to Clurman that they should organize a workshop where raw talents like Brando could be nurtured, where actors and directors could experiment endlessly and privately, and where they could fail, because you have to fail in order to succeed, failures in art being just as important as success. Kazan eventually discussed the concept in more detail with the director Robert Lewis as they strolled through Central Park.

By the following year the Actors Studio had begun classes, taught by Lewis and Kazan in a dingy room on the top floor of the Old Labor Stage at Broadway and Twenty-ninth Street. At the first meeting, movie star and former Group Theatre member John Garfield greeted people at the door: Julie Harris, Maureen Stapleton, Shelley Winters, Marlon Brando, Kevin McCarthy, David Wayne, Anne Jackson, Montgomery Clift, and Eli Wallach were some of the young talents who crowded in to hear Kazan announce that he'd invited them all there for a reason: He wanted to create a new generation of actors and maybe create a common language for everybody.

"This is not a club, this is a gym for actors to work out in. Everybody is expected to work hard." And if they didn't, they wouldn't be asked back, he told them brusquely.

The Actors Studio was founded at the start of the Cold War, at the time of the Truman Doctrine and the establishment of the CIA. The extraordinary energy of its first stars was both a protest and a hope for the future. As Kazan saw it, his task at the studio was to "turn psychology into behavior." He would always have a commitment to emotional and physical naturalism. He longed to get away from "actorish" performances, and he did that both in theater and in film, especially when he was on location in such places as New Orleans or Mississippi. His job, as he saw it, "was not simply to entertain but to leave the audience with something so vivid when they went home that it could change their lives."

Meanwhile Hollywood was making offers to Brando. He agreed to do a screen test but showed his contempt by playing with a yo-yo throughout. He was completely indifferent to his growing fame. He sensed he was not the usual leading man type. He didn't think he fitted into any category.

His actor friends applauded him for not "selling out" to films. He was going to be their god; he was going to be their leader. Everybody in Stella's class thought so, and to young New York actors, plays were still what mattered, the theater was what mattered, although the theater no longer dominated Broadway; movies did. Now it was moviegoers who thronged Times Square and packed into the huge palaces like the Capitol and the Paramount. Even Brando attended more movies than plays. He especially loved the classics he could see at the Museum of Modern Art, such as the Chaplin films and Jean Renoir's *Grand Illusion*.

Still, he did see theater, like the hit play *Life with Father* and the musical *Oklahoma!*, and he'd already made an effort to catch Montgomery Clift in Lillian Hellman's *The Searching Wind*, because Clift was the rival juvenile, and he wanted to check him out. He thought Clift was terrific. After the show Brando went backstage to tell him so. They became casual friends. Both had been born in Omaha, but the similarity ended there. Clift was brooding, reserved, and a terrific technician. He'd been a child actor, and he was enormously ambitious. Brando was sensual and increasingly boorish. He often seemed to view his involvement with acting as a joke.

Interestingly enough, Montgomery Clift went to Hollywood before Brando, in 1948, and became the first alienated rebel hero in the western *Red River*, in which he gets beaten to a pulp by John Wayne. Then Brando took over and became the prototype of the 1950s macho outsider, the American male who cares so deeply he must pretend not to care at all.

While the two of them were in New York, they often showed up at the same parties. "It was wild to see them together," says Kevin McCarthy. "Monty was so buttoned down and elegant, and Marlon was always trying to get a rise out of him, and Monty would ignore him. Once Marlon joked, 'What's the matter with Monty Clift? He acts like he has a Mixmaster up his ass and he doesn't want anyone to know about it.'" No one could figure Brando out. Did he care about acting? Was he trying to put something over on people? What was he going to do next?

Guthrie McClintic, the eminent producer-director, who'd seen Brando in *Truckline Cafe*, thought he would make a wonderful Marchbanks for his wife, Katherine Cornell, in Shaw's *Candida*. Brando was intimidated by the thought of acting in a play opposite Cornell, "the American Duse." At that point Broadway was a matriarchy, with great actresses like Helen Hayes, Ruth Gordon, and Judith Anderson dominating the boards. Brando was scared. But Stella Adler urged him to take up the challenge, and so did Dodie when he spoke to her on the phone.

Those who saw him as Marchbanks never forgot him. Actress Terry Hayden recalls how strange and shy he was onstage. He had a hunted, tormented manner. He wore a ragged jacket and sneakers—his costume choices—and he leaped over a sofa to kneel at Cornell's feet. You completely believed he was a sensitive young poet in love with an older woman, Hayden says.

Their appearance together had some historical significance, since Brando was to epitomize mid-century psychological naturalism onstage, whereas Cornell was the ultimate old-fashioned theatrical grande dame. She used extravagant gestures and a thrilling vibrato, what amounted to an exalted romanticism. He wrote his sister Frannie that "Cornell is very beautiful but there is a nebulous quality about her acting I find hard to relate to—acting with her is like trying to bite down on a tomato seed." Even so, for twenty-four performances, the stage of the Cort proved not just a haven for the nervous young poet Marchbanks reading his sonnets to his beloved Candida, but a meeting ground for theater that was passing and theater that was yet to come.

Critics called his performance effective because it was so restrained and real. He was vastly relieved when it was over.

Meanwhile he was starting to attract attention offstage. Truman Capote described his "squat gymnasium physique—the weight lifter's arms, the Charles Atlas chest"—but it "was as if a stranger's head had been attached to the brawny body." The face was a poet's face, gentle and angelic, refined: the eyes, warm and sad; the mouth, almost womanly.

"He was like a magnetic field," Sondra Lee said. "Everyone was drawn to him—men, women, animals—and he didn't know how to deal with it."

"There was this quality of something always withheld, so he created this mystique, and we didn't really make an effort to crack the shell," adds actor Freddie Sadoff. Sadoff, along with Sondra Lee, singer Janice Mars, and actors Carlo Fiore, Billy Redfield, and Maureen Stapleton, among others, was part of a ragtag group that followed Brando all around Manhattan "like he was the Pied Piper." Sometimes they went up to Harlem to listen to jazz, usually with the black actor William Greaves leading the way.

Otherwise they used to cram into Wally Cox's West Fifty-seventh Street apartment, which he was sharing with Brando. The door was always open. Often up to fifteen people could be seen milling aimlessly around the room, "like it was a bus station," someone said. "Everyone doing his thing," Maureen Stapleton remembered. "A couple might be playing chess. Some girl might be eating an apple by the window."

Wrote Janice Mars in a letter to Brando years later: "Flouting all conventions, we were like orphans in rebellion against everything. None of us had emotionally secure family backgrounds so we gravitated to each other and created a family among ourselves. We were a mutual support system and we accepted each other's foibles, faults and all."

"Marlon was our leader, the common denominator," Sondra Lee said. "He'd move around the room, drawing one person after another into a corner, and talking conspiratorially with them one-on-one. He made you feel as if you were the most important person in the world. Marlon had separate groups of friends," she went on, "and he kept them separate. There were the strays, and there were the oddballs, and there were the intellectuals like Harold and Stella, who were his mentors and who he revered, and then there were the special ones really close to him, like Celia and Wally." Most of these people have remained his friends throughout his life. He stayed in contact with them for the next four decades, unless, like Carlo Fiore, they wrote tell-all books about him or talked about him to the press. Then they were dropped, and he never spoke to them again.

He told Truman Capote he made friends warily, circling them, moving in, then moving back. "They don't know what's happening," he said. "Before they realize it, they're all entangled, involved. I have them. And suddenly, sometimes I'm all *they* have. ...But I want to help them, and they can focus on me."

Brando's women, who were starting to be legion, were in and out of the apartment at all hours: Hispanic, Asian, dark-skinned, exotic, temperamental, usually beautiful, although a few were not. "Marlon sometimes took pity on really homely girls," his grandmother Nana commented. "Girls with crossed eyes, overweight girls..."

According to Mars, Brando preferred older women. "He was looking for a substitute mother," she said, and he had "a perverse need to humiliate to see how far a female would go to indulge him.... For Marlon, sex had as much significance as eating a chocolate bar or taking an aspirin."

At the time Brando fantasized about having a "harem of girls—a fat pink one I could chase around the room and pinch, one for roller skating, one for an afternoon in a barn, all kinds of girls, all shapes, all colorings..."

After *Candida* closed, Brando had only a brief respite before starting rehearsals for *A Flag Is Born,* by Ben Hecht, about refugees trying to get into the Holy Land. Paul Muni starred; Luther Adler directed. The drama, which was really propaganda for establishing a Jewish homeland in the Middle East, was produced by the American League for a Free Palestine.

Brando was thrilled to be working with Muni. He had seen all his movies, and he believed he was one of the greatest actors in the world (he still holds that view) because Muni had no identifiable "image" on the screen. Brando marveled at his ability to disguise himself. As the gangster in *Scarface,* the Chinese coolie in *The Good Earth,* the novelist Émile Zola who championed Dreyfus, he always wore a mask. Stella Adler once explained that Muni's work expressed the rich theatrical tradition honed in the Yiddish theater (of which he was an alumnus). "Being versatile is much more admired than being a 'personality.'"

In *A Flag Is Born,* Brando played a cynical young Jew who at the end of the play has a show-stopping speech in which he addresses the audience directly and shouts, "You let six million people die!" He vows he will fight to achieve the refugees' dream of emigrating to the Jewish homeland. Every night he brought down the house with his passion.

The success of *A Flag Is Born* was unexpected. The three-week run extended to three months. He left the show before it closed, but he went on raising money for the cause, making speeches at synagogues all over Manhattan and Long Island. He was totally caught up in the idea of a homeland for the Jews, and for a while he was a passionate Zionist. Years later he started speaking out for the Palestinians.

Early in 1947, Brando played opposite Tallulah Bankhead, one of Broadway's most temperamental stars, in Jean Cocteau's *The Eagle Has Two Heads*. Rehearsals were difficult, and he was fired out of town, mainly because he constantly upstaged Bankhead during performances, by squirming, picking his nose, adjusting his fly, leering at the audience, even mooning for a full minute, the press agent Richard Maney noted. Brando also chewed garlic before he had to kiss Bankhead in the love scenes. "I avoided her tongue as best I could," he told a friend. "For some reason her tongue was especially cold." He wrote to his sister, "I would rather be dragged over broken crockery than make love to Tallulah."

Going back to New York, he fell asleep on the train, and his wallet was stolen. He returned to his shabby apartment feeling blue and vaguely embarrassed about being an actor. Although he admired Stella Adler's ideas about the theater as art, he still wasn't sure acting was something a real man should do. But what else was he suited for?

Now he was out of work. He had a little money saved, and

he would help his less fortunate friends with rent and food. When someone needed shock therapy, he paid for that. He paid for a great many abortions. "Marlon was at his best when he was called on to take care of someone. He liked to be needed," said Sondra Lee. "He seemed acutely aware of everybody's pain." He was terrified that he might someday become dependent on liquor, as his parents were, possibly explaining why he gorged on peanut butter and junk food whenever he was depressed. Above all, he confided to Sondra, he didn't want to be a mama's boy.

He continued to kid around. Sometimes he would throw horse turds from his apartment window on passersby, and he and some of his fellow actors shoplifted regularly from Woolworth's. Early in the fall of 1947 he and Wally Cox moved to a tenement floor-through on West Fifty-second Street and Tenth Avenue. It was furnished with mattresses on the floor, piles of books, a wind instrument, Wally's electric trains, and Brando's drums. They both had motorcycles—Wally had taught Brando how to ride one—and they zoomed around the city, dropping in on friends, often in the dead of night.

They also gave their first dinner party. Shelley Winters, who was dating Brando at the time, was their only guest. She recalls Brando's doing push-ups in an old gray sweatshirt while Wally prepared the meal: "rice with nuts, cauliflower in sour cream, and for dessert fried grapefruit. White wine spiked with gin was served in cracked old mugs."

4

"DEAR POP," BRANDO WROTE his father in September 1947, "I start rehearsals Oct. 4th for a 'Streetcar Named Desire.' I'm getting $550 [a week] and second billing. Elia Kazan is directing. The female lead—Jessica Tandy. Karl Malden plays supporting role. It's a strong, violent, sincere play—emotional rather than intellectual impact."

He did not elaborate on the tragic, poetic grandeur of the play, written by Tennessee Williams, whose earlier work *A Glass Menagerie* had won the New York Drama Critics Circle Award. Nor did he mention that he'd won the role of Stanley Kowalski over John Garfield and Burt Lancaster.

Brando had not auditioned formally but had instead dropped by Kazan's cluttered office at 1545 Broadway for a talk. Kazan (nicknamed Gadg) disliked auditions: "They never work, because you don't see the quality of the person." A former actor himself and possibly the greatest actor's director who ever lived, he once explained his technique to writer Jeff Young: "Before I start with anybody in an important role, I talk with them for a long time, and before you know it they are telling me about their mothers and their infidelities—anything they feel guilty about." Kazan preferred to sit over coffee and gently shoot the breeze with an actor. A master of charm and manipulation, he could usually get anyone to open up.

But Brando held back, and Kazan noted the unsettled stillness about him and decided he was probably a troubled soul. He had not forgotten the impact he'd made in *Truckline Cafe;* the overwhelming effect of his angry sexual presence was powerful.

Part of Kazan's genius as a director was that he always matched the character of the play with the emotional core of the actor. Earlier he had cast James Dunn in his movie *A Tree Grows in Brooklyn,* not because he was such a good actor, but because he was an alcoholic trying to go on the wagon and he had the reformed drunk's sense of guilt.

Kazan saw in Brando the characteristics of Stanley: the sexual magnetism, the brooding self-involvement, the little-boy quality. He was both brute and infant, and he had a strange tenderness, as well as a bizarre sense of humor Kazan hoped to tap.

That day in the director's office, the two men spoke briefly, Kazan doing most of the talking in short, impatient bursts. "The central motif of *Streetcar,* the central conflict," he said, "is desire and sensitivity versus brutality. It's about the outcast in the society, the poet, the crazy lady. But if Stanley is cruel to Blanche, it's because she's trying to take over his apartment, his turf. He's trying to save his balls."

Brando had already read the play and privately decided the part of Stanley was "too large" for him. After they had spoken for a few minutes, Kazan told him the role could be his; did he want it? Brando mumbled he'd have to think about it. In the next days he tried to phone Kazan to tell him no, but the line was always busy. Then Kazan phoned him and demanded, "You wanna do it, Marlon?" and Brando found himself saying yes. The next thing he knew, Kazan had arranged a meeting for him with Tennessee Williams in Provincetown.

The sleepy-eyed playwright was vacationing on the Cape with his lover Pancho and his good friend Margo Jones, head of Houston's Alley Theatre. Kazan gave Brando the bus fare, which he promptly spent on food (he was hungry and broke). He had to hitchhike to Provincetown with his favorite girlfriend, Celia Webb, and arrived two days late. The sun had just set.

They found Williams and his friends half drunk in a little shack on the beach. The place was in total darkness. "Something happened to the lights," the playwright drawled. "And the plumbing isn't working either." Brando went around fixing the fuses and unclogging the toilet. Then he sat down on the couch, and with Williams cueing him as Blanche, Brando read a few of Stanley's key speeches from *Streetcar*. The effect on everyone was instantaneous. Margo Jones let out a Texas whoop and yelled, "Get Kazan on the phone! That is the greatest reading I ever heard!"

Afterward Williams wrote his agent, Audrey Wood: "I can't tell you what a relief it is that we have found such a God-sent Stanley in the person of Brando. It had not occurred to me before what an excellent value would come through casting a very young actor in this part. It humanizes the character of Stanley in that it becomes the brutality or callousness of youth rather than a vicious older man.... Brando's reading...was by far the best reading I have ever heard. He seemed to have already created a dimensional character, of the sort that the war has produced among young veterans."

Forty years later Harold Brodkey in *The New Yorker* added, "Brando's new take on the working-class father of the country was a very important cultural invention.... He was in many ways a kind of unknown soldier—not dead, but dead-souled as a result of the Second World War."

That evening up in Provincetown, everyone ate takeout. Then Williams read some poetry and sucked on a hygienic cigarette holder full of absorbent crystals; a vague smile played on his face. Around midnight Brando and Celia Webb wrapped themselves in a quilt and fell asleep on the floor while the others retired to bunk beds.

The following morning Brando asked Williams to go for a walk on the beach, "And I did," the playwright recalls in his memoir. Together they strolled across the dunes as small waves lapped near their bare feet. "We returned to the house in silence," Williams goes on. "Marlon and I never exchanged a word about the play or anything else. But," he adds, "I had never seen a man of such extraordinary beauty." Later that day Williams loaned Brando and Celia bus fare so they could return to New York.

Once back in the city, Brando did read for Kazan, who was having second thoughts about Brando's unpredictable acting methods, even though Williams insisted he had both the humanity and the eccentricity that Stanley required. In September, Jessica Tandy, who by now had been cast as the doomed Blanche DuBois, and Brando read through the script under Kazan's steady guidance. He'd also hired twenty-one-year-old Kim Hunter as Stanley's pregnant wife, Stella, and Karl Malden was to play Stanley's buddy, Mitch.

Rehearsals started in the ghostly confines of the New Amsterdam Roof Theater, a slanting, dusty space atop an office building on West Forty-second Street. During the 1920s Florenz Ziegfeld had staged midnight musical revues here. Kazan often rehearsed his shows at the New Amsterdam because it was private and nobody nosed around, except for Shelley Winters, who was still dating Brando and hovered in the wings until Kazan barked, "Don't just stand there, Shel, get us some coffee!"

The cast, with producer Irene Selznick, gathered around a table, and Kazan introduced everybody. Brando, in khakis and grimy shirt, kept mumbling, "John Garfield should be doing this part, not me." Tennessee Williams was there too, trying to put names to faces, when Kazan announced, "There will be no rewrites. The dialogue is frozen." The playwright let loose with a piercing cackle and informed the group that this would be his last play because he was dying of pancreatic cancer and had no more energy for more work. The actors didn't know how to respond. However, Williams and Kazan went on to collaborate on four more projects: *Cat on a Hot Tin Roof, Sweet Bird of Youth, Camino Real,* and *Baby Doll.*

That first week Kazan focused on the relationships within *Streetcar,* which he described as a "poetic tragedy." He did a great many improvisations, with the actors playing their characters in imaginary scenes before the action of the play began. Some of the improvs were done in order to break

Tandy from her rigid Royal Academy habits of acting. "I wanted her to be more vulnerable," Kazan says. Once he even tied her up in ropes and had the rest of the cast make fun of her. "I did all kinds of things in those days to make her feel helpless or whatever the hell I wanted her to be," he adds.

Brando didn't improvise on Stanley. Kazan told Jeff Young, "His experience was so rich you just had to call attention to what it was you wanted. He even listened experientially. It was as if you were playing on something. He didn't look at you, and he hardly acknowledged what you were saying. He was tuned into you, without listening to you intellectually or mentally. It was a mysterious process. I knew him so well in those days that I'd say very little to him, and it would turn on a whole mess of things within him."

But Brando, undisciplined and moody, remained an enigma to the rest of the cast. After a week he brought a cot to the theater and slept there. Once he disappeared and returned very late to rehearsal. He was pale and unshaven. Irene Selznick recalled that Kazan "put his arms around Marlon. It was extraordinary to see so tough a man as Gadg so tender. Gadg gave him some money and sent him out to eat."

Brando was having genuine difficulty with the role. He could not seem to memorize his lines. He appeared depressed and anxious. At one point he was so inaudible that Jessica Tandy lashed out at him. "Speak up! I can't hear a bloody word you're saying." He apologized, but for a while things didn't improve. Theirs was a prickly relationship at best, and Kazan used it to the play's advantage.

To help his concentration, Kazan taught Brando how to play with props, objects that could convey character and feelings and were symbolic of something, like the cold beer Stanley keeps swigging with such gusto, the cigar he keeps sucking on instead of a teat. (Later Brando became a master at using objects to convey emotion, like the glove in *On the Waterfront* and the cat he stroked so gently as the sinister Mafia Godfather.)

Between rehearsals Kazan had him train with weights, and he insisted that he diet and learn to box. "Stanley gloried in his body; it took his mind off his supreme dissatisfaction." Slowly, as he gained in confidence, Brando began developing the swagger he felt he needed for Stanley, the air of defiance. "All of a sudden he began copying Gadg's swagger," Brando's longtime makeup man, Phil Rhodes, recalls.

By then the director was allowing Brando into his own life a bit. They had dropped by the Actors Studio once or twice, and Brando had taken note of Kazan's various girlfriends. And on their walks around the city after rehearsal, he occasionally was invited to stop by Kazan's brownstone on the East Side, where he met Molly, the director's plain, long-suffering wife. Brando also baby-sat Kazan's little son, Nick.

Kazan was a bitter, potent, philandering man, and as rehearsals intensified, Brando psyched him out, absorbing his posture, his glances, his walk. Whether or not the director ever caught on or cared is subject to debate, although he did write in his *Streetcar* journal, "Stanley (M.B.) like E.K. is self-absorbed to the point of fascination."

Finally, near the third week of rehearsal, Brando got a bead on the character when the costume designer, Lucinda Ballard, took him for a fitting at the Eaves Costume Company. As Peter Manso tells the story in his monumental biography,

Brando, she'd decided to dress him like one of the Con Ed ditch diggers she'd seen slaving away in the heat in midtown. "Their clothes were so dirty that they had stuck to their bodies." Ballard hit upon an "undesigned" outfit—T-shirt and blue jeans—that ultimately became part of the Brando iconography, the new symbol of American maleness, the decade's biggest fashion symbol.

She dyed a couple of T-shirts red and washed them over and over again until they had shrunk. Then she tore the right shoulder to suggest that Stella might have scratched Stanley. She had the tailor cut and taper the jeans to fit the contours of Brando's body like a second skin; they were tight as a glove, and Brando didn't wear any underpants when he was fitted. When he saw his reflection in the mirror, he saw how the jeans outlined every muscle in his thighs. He "almost went crazy," Ballard told Peter Manso. "He was dancing between the glass cases...leaping up off the ground. Brando said, 'This is it! This is what I've always wanted!'"

Next he had his blond hair as well as his lashes and brows dyed brown, and the transformation of Brando into Stanley Kowalski was complete. It was as if the costume had released him emotionally.

From then on Brando's instincts took him all sorts of places in rehearsals, as in the famous birthday party scene in which he stormed from the table, then slammed his hand down on his plate, smashing it to smithereens. As he delivered his line "My place is cleared. You want me to clear your places?" he swept the rest of the plates from the table with a great crash. The first time he played the scene full out, he had to keep picking shards of china from his bloodied fingers, but he spoke his lines anyway. He was totally into his character.

Later he told Pat Cox (Wally Cox's wife) how he found "Stanley's voice. I'm an ear man, you know." He had actually heard the voice in his head. When he first came to New York, he'd sit in the Optima cigar store phone booth on Forty-second Street, watching the tourists move up and down Times Square. He loved observing people, listening to them cough and spit and yak: "Hey, whatcha doin'? Wanna hot dog?"

These sounds—flat, nasal, mocking—became the aural memories he drew on as he figured out the kind of diction and voice placement for Stanley. Bit by bit, he discovered vocal mannerisms for the scripted words in order to express the tensions of an inarticulate man. He said later that his image for Stanley was partly drawn from his Times Square observations too. He would watch guys in nylon shirts on their way to the Automat or the porn shows, "guys like Stanley, who hold a cup of coffee like an animal with a paw around it. The Stanleys of the world have no self-awareness."

At the final run-through of *Streetcar,* both Kazan and Williams were staggered by the untutored sensitivity Brando was bringing to the role. Stella Adler and Hume Cronin (Tandy's husband) attended the run-through. Cronin expressed concern that "Jessie could do better" and asked Kazan please to keep on encouraging her. Kazan knew then that Brando's volcanic performance was shifting the balance of the play, and the sympathy was going to Stanley, not Blanche.

Kazan was worried that Williams would be upset, but on the contrary, Williams was thrilled. "Marlon's a genius," he crowed. "Let him be." To Williams, Brando's Stanley was an early version of the midnight cowboy, a

Lawrencian fantasy of the earthy proletarian male.

On opening night in New Haven the show was a technical shambles. The complex lighting system didn't work. Music cues were off. But when Brando entered as Blanche DuBois's brutal executioner, in his jeans and T-shirt, clutching his bloody package of meat, the audience gasped.

After the curtain had come down, Irene Selznick gave a party in her suite at the Taft Hotel. Arthur Miller dropped by. Kazan had invited him, and the lanky playwright said he'd been "enthralled" by the extraordinary sense of language of the play, its freedom, the poetry in the dialogue. He was so inspired that after the party he went back to New York and immediately finished *Death of a Salesman*.

The playwright Thornton Wilder, author of *The Skin of Our Teeth*, dropped by too; he was teaching at Yale. He primly gave his critique of *Streetcar;* it was negative. He maintained that the play was based on a totally false premise. No southern belle as genteel as Stella would marry a brute like Stanley, let alone succumb to his sexual violence. Tennessee Williams listened politely for as long as he could, but when Wilder was out of earshot, he murmured, "That man has never had a good lay!"

After four more sold-out performances, the play moved to Boston and then Philadelphia, where the reaction was the same: raves for Marlon Brando.

A Streetcar Named Desire opened on December 3, 1947, at the Barrymore Theater on Broadway. Notables from New York and Hollywood packed the house to watch Brando, as Stanley, proceed to trap Jessica Tandy's faded southern belle, Blanche DuBois, and force her to confront her nymphomania, her alcoholism, her pathetic dreams. The audience in that theater sensed they were witnessing the dawn of a new cultural era, a breakdown of sexual taboos; the play's central conflict, of desire and sensitivity against brutality, dramatized the eternal clash within everyone.

When the curtain came down, the entire audience stood and applauded for a full half hour, until Kazan, rumpled and frowning, jumped up onstage and was joined by Tennessee Williams, who was so undone that he bowed to the cast and forgot about the cheering behind him.

An excited little mob crowded into Brando's dressing room. Wally Cox found his friend sorting through telegrams. One of them was from Williams, and it read, "RIDE OUT BOY AND SEND IT SOLID. FROM THE GREASY POLACK YOU WILL SOME DAY ARRIVE AT THE GLOOMY DANE FOR YOU HAVE SOMETHING THAT MAKES THE THEATRE A WORLD OF GREAT POSSIBILITIES."

Brando's performance was to revolutionize the craft of acting. With *Streetcar,* he had delivered something uncomfortable and dangerous. "Marlon Brando, mumbling, muttering, flashing with barbaric energy, freed theatrical emotion from its enslavement by words," declared Camille Paglia later. "Brando brought American nature to American acting, and he brought the American personality to the world.... Brando, the wild, sexy rebel, all mute and surly bad attitude, prefigured the great art form of the Sixties generation: rock and roll."

Back in 1949, audiences who saw Brando onstage as Stanley saw something that was without precedent. "It was an experience to watch with what chameleon ease Marlon acquired Stanley's cruel, gaudy colors," Truman Capote wrote, "how like a guileful salamander he slithered into the part and his own persona evaporated."

He always played moment to moment. To keep everything fresh, he would add, change, adjust. Kim Hunter recalled, "It was exciting to work with him. Some nights he made terrible choices but they were always *real*. That's why it was such a challenge."

All the more so because he never liked the character he was playing. In his autobiography he writes, "I was the antithesis of Stanley Kowalski. I was sensitive by nature and he was coarse." He adds, "I think Jessica and I were miscast, and between us we threw the play out of balance. Jessica is a very good actress, but I never thought she was believable as Blanche. I didn't think she had the finesse or cultivated femininity that the part required.... Blanche DuBois was a shattered butterfly, soft and delicate.... [Jessica] was too shrill to elicit the sympathy and pity that the woman deserved-....People laughed at me at certain points in the play, turning Blanche into a foolish character....I didn't try to make Stanley funny. People simply laughed, and Jessica...really disliked me for it, although I've always suspected that in her heart she must have known it wasn't my fault."

Two years later, in the movie version of *Streetcar*, the English actress Vivien Leigh took *Streetcar* back from Brando's Stanley in a performance of harrowing power and beauty. Brando was the first to admit that.

After *Streetcar* opened on Broadway, fame overwhelmed Brando. Hollywood offers poured in. He was photographed by Cecil Beaton for *Vogue*. *Time, Life, Look,* and *Theatre Arts* interviewed him. "He tried to be amiable and dignified with reporters," said Irving Schneider, Irene Selznick's associate.

"But Marlon often behaved as if he was half asleep when he was talking. His voice sounded unemotional and boyish, and he'd ramble on and on. He was very self-involved."

He was still living with Wally Cox in filth and squalor, still playing with electric trains and eating peanut butter out of a jar. He said years afterward that he wasn't *aware* he was successful. How could he be receiving so much praise and money when Pop had told him he would never amount to a tinker's damn? He would wander the streets late at night and not *see* anything. He kept wondering whether acting was really what he wanted to do. Then, after a couple of months, he told Truman Capote, "I began to hear this roar....All right. You're a *success*, at least you're *accepted*, and welcomed everywhere, but that's it.... That's all there is to it, and it doesn't lead anywhere. You're just sitting on top of a pile of candy, gathering thick layers of *crust*."

Early in 1948 he paid a surprise weekend visit to his parents. They'd just moved to another farm outside Libertyville.

A great deal had happened to them in the past year. Dodie had not only joined AA but become a terrific spokesperson for the organization. She had "qualified," which was still unusual for a woman to do in the 1940s, to admit frankly that she'd been an alcoholic. She spoke eloquently in the meetings about her years as a falling-down drunk. Senior was also in AA. They had patched up their marriage and seemed to be living together quite amicably. Brando noted Dodie now dressed mostly in jeans and worked in her garden, smoking endless cigarettes. She read voluminously and dabbled in spiritualism.

Nobody ever knew how Brando felt about his mother's recovery from alcoholism. He did not mention her recovery; he would refer to her mournfully as a "drunk" and as the mother he'd repeatedly had to save when he was a teenager. Possibly he felt less needed by her now that she was sober, and this upset him, although he didn't realize it. He always said his panic attacks had increased, as had his periods of depression, "after my mother left me in New York." He didn't add, "after she joined AA."

Dodie of course was thrilled by Brando's huge success on Broadway. He'd succeeded in the theater; he was a fulfillment of her own dreams. And Senior seemed proud that Bud was finally "amounting to something," although he "still didn't understand the boy at all."

Brando hoped they could develop a better relationship. So when his father suggested Brando turn his weekly paycheck of $550 over to him to invest, he agreed, although he didn't really want to give Senior his money since he knew he was a bad businessman. But he was afraid to tell him that. Besides, in spite of his grown-up success, he clung to a postadolescent lifestyle: He was almost always broke because he kept lending cash to less fortunate friends. So Brando did mail Senior his check every week, and Senior mailed him back an allowance, invested the rest, and they both avoided discussing it.

Senior was actually embarrassed by his son's new financial power. He got edgy when people would ask his name, and he'd say, "Marlon Brando," and they'd respond, "But *you're* not Marlon Brando, the actor," and he'd tell them sadly, "No, I'm Marlon Brando's *father*."

*

In the next year, success and fame began causing Brando a great many problems. His anxiety attacks increased. He couldn't sleep, and he had bowel trouble. He suffered excruciating headaches. Sometimes if he was recognized in a cab, he'd scrunch down in the seat and deny he was Marlon Brando. On the street he often fled from girls who ran after him. He hated being singled out at restaurants and nightclubs.

Once he confided to Maureen Stapleton that he was terrified he might kill someone, hurt someone when he went into a rage. Stapleton says, "Marlon had no idea where his rage was coming from, but he was very frightened of it." He decided to talk to Kazan. The director suggested Brando see his own analyst, Bela Mittelmann, whose specialty was psychosomatic illnesses. "I think Marlon found Mittelmann uncritical enough so that he could talk to him," Kazan recalled to Brando biographer Peter Manso.

He went to Mittelmann religiously for the next eleven years, five days a week, when he was in New York. He told his friends about Mittelmann. "Everybody knew...that he was a big force in his life," Sondra Lee said. "When something would come up...he'd say, 'I'll have to talk to Mittelmann....'"

The next decade became the psychoanalytic era: Everyone started seeing a shrink. Pat Cox said, "We were all terribly self-conscious about it. You no longer said, 'What's the matter with you?' You said, 'You're not relating to me.'" During the 1950s "society was moved not by injustice but by penis envy, patricidal anxieties, incestuous yearnings, and suppressed homosexuality," wrote Arthur Miller mockingly in a landmark essay, "The Year It Came Apart." "Now guilt was personal again and for many the age-old battle with public evils became the last illusion. I am because I am guilty."

Nowhere was this truer than at the Actors Studio, home of the Method, which stressed actors' real-life experiences. "Draw on them, turn trauma into drama," Kazan was heard to say. It was even pointed out that Freud had started his studies in the subconscious, into dreams, at the same time Stanislavsky was codifying his system for actors, linking the actor's physical behavior with his inner life, his spirit.

However, during the run of *Streetcar*, when Brando attended Bobby Lewis's class at the studio, he discovered that Lewis wasn't stressing the psychological; he was stressing the classics. He had the students analyzing Chekhov and Shakespeare and talking about intention and style. He wanted Brando to stretch himself in a role he might not ordinarily be cast in. "I didn't want him to use himself as much as I wanted him to use his actor's imagination," he said. He suggested that Brando do a scene from Robert Sherwood's *Reunion in Vienna*, playing the archduke Rudolf Maximilian von Hapsburg. The part had been brilliantly portrayed by Alfred Lunt on Broadway during the 1930s.

Lewis added he must bring in "a complete physical characterization—full uniform, sword, monocle, Viennese accent, the whole bit." Brando reluctantly agreed. He began studying Velázquez portraits of the "Hapsburg lip." He tried to figure out the kind of mustache he should wear. He was soon practicing with a monocle, popping it in and out of his eye, and he chose the music to play beforehand—Viennese waltzes.

Backstage at the Barrymore Theater, where they shared a

dressing room, Brando discussed with Karl Malden what he hoped to do. Malden recalls, "Marlon kept trying to figure out how he could show that this once-privileged and rich Rudolf was now so broke he was driving a cab. He kept racking his brain to come up with a solution, but he never told me what he planned to do."

He rehearsed and procrastinated for weeks. Finally came the day for performing the scene with actress Joan Chandler, who was playing the elegant lady whose love the archduke wants to rekindle. Brando made his entrance to a standing-room-only class, most of whom had only seen him play the vulgarian Stanley in T-shirt and jeans. Now he was in full princely regalia: brocaded uniform, sword clanking, a monocle, a pencil-thin mustache. He sat down and removed one boot, revealing a sock with a big hole in it. He attempted to stretch his sock over the toe to cover the hole; then he sighed and put the boot back on. "It was pure Marlon," Karl Malden remembers. "Simple and brilliant, communicating everything we had to know about the character's economic straits."

Midway through the scene, Brando had to seduce Chandler. Suddenly he marched across the stage, slapped her silly, and then kissed her with great passion, ad-libbing, "Have you ever been kissed like that before?" The students roared with laughter. With that, Brando really took off, pouring champagne down her bodice as she screamed and struggled. He completed the scene in high good humor and with an impeccable Viennese accent.

The class cheered, although there were disagreements afterward. Karl Malden wrote in his autobiography, "Some of us weren't sure that what Marlon had done to Joan was fair.

He had humiliated and hurt her. Were we laughing at the situation in the play, or what Marlon had done to her as an actor?" Bobby Lewis thought that was irrelevant: "All's fair in art," he commented in his memoir, *Slings and Arrows*. "Marlon proved to us he could do anything. He gave a hilarious light comedy performance that's remembered to this day."

For the next two years Brando needed all the diversion he could find. The emotional grind of playing the same part night after night was driving him crazy. He writes in his autobiography:

> Try to imagine what it was like walking on a stage at 8:30 every night having to yell, scream, cry, break dishes, kick the furniture, punch the walls and *experience* the same intense, wrenching emotions night after night....It was exhausting. Then imagine what it was like to walk off the stage after pulling those emotions out of yourself knowing you had to do it all over again a few hours later....There was a fundamental part of me that was determined not to fail as Stanley Kowalski, to excel and be the best, so I applied pressure on myself to act the part well every time. But it was emotionally draining...and after a few weeks I wanted out of it. I couldn't quit, however, because I had a run-of-the-play contract.

His performances varied widely. Sometimes he could be electrifying, but sometimes he walked through the show or arrived so late he missed entrance cues, and he made the actors so angry they ad-libbed, hoping to throw him. He was always able to turn the tables on them with an impromptu remark. During the twenty minutes he was offstage, he would become bored and restless, so he'd work out with weights to keep his phenomenal body glistening with muscle. Sometimes he would quickly make love to a girl in his dressing room, or he'd box with his understudy, Jack Palance, and members of the cast and crew. He was not a very good fighter, and one night a stagehand slammed his fist into Brando and broke his nose. He played the rest of the show with a bloody handkerchief pressed against his face. Tandy was furious. "You bloody fool!" she snarled.

They were at each other constantly. "Marlon couldn't stand Jessie, and he was always out to bug her," says Phil Rhodes. One afternoon the stage manager received a phone call from someone warning that Jessica Tandy would be shot if she appeared onstage that night. Soon detectives were swarming the theater, but the show went on. Tandy was her usual dazzling professional self, and nothing happened. But Karl Malden wondered if Brando hadn't made the anonymous threat. "Marlon loved playing cruel practical jokes. He especially loved it when he could pull off a prank in complete secrecy."

Nobody ever found out if he'd been responsible, but he was responsible for putting dog shit in the food onstage, and he also urged a group of drunken sailors he'd run into on Forty-second Street to visit Tandy backstage after the show; she'd be sexually available, he said. The sailors did show up but were kept from entering the theater.

Years afterward Tandy commented dryly, "There were many, many times when I wanted to wring Marlon Brando's little neck."

He couldn't seem to help himself. After the show he'd do

crazy things like hang out the window of his apartment until his friends screamed in terror and he pulled himself back, laughing wildly. He enjoyed breaking into and entering other people's houses, friends' places, to borrow a book or maybe just to sleep in a clean bed for a change. Writer Bob Condon, then in advertising, remembers Brando used to climb through his kitchen window into his flat to use the orange juice squeezer. Then he'd "drink the juice and steal away out the window into the dawn. Several times overnight guests would scream as the window slid open and then stare open-mouthed as Brando crept over the sill."

Then there was the time he attended an elegant little soiree Leila Hadley (now Mrs. Henry Luce III) gave for Irwin Shaw. "S. J. Perelman was there. So was Al Hirschfeld and Gloria Vanderbilt. Marlon was the only newcomer to the party, so he stood out. He would have stood out anyway, he was so gorgeous. I noticed him eyeing my collection of miniature antique clocks. Then I forgot about him and tended to my guests."

The next day Leila realized that her antique clocks were missing, and she immediately sensed that Brando had pocketed them. She phoned his agent, Edie Van Cleve, and explained that the clocks had disappeared, and they were family heirlooms. She didn't say Brando had taken them; she just said he'd been at the party and "might know where they were." After a couple of minutes the agent called her back. "I passed along the information to Marlon," she said.

That evening Leila's collection of miniature antique clocks was lined up outside her apartment door with a note in a childish scrawl: "Oops! (Signed) a thief."

Brando remained close to his sisters, especially Jocelyn. By 1948 she was having her biggest success as the only woman in the Broadway hit *Mister Roberts,* starring Henry Fonda. Brando was extremely pleased about that, and he was anxious that Wally Cox have some success as well. Cox was still eking out an existence making intricate silver jewelry with Dick Loving, who ultimately married Brando's younger sister, Frannie.

"Wally meant more to him than any other person in the world, woman or man," Pat Cox, Wally's third wife, would say. During the run of *Streetcar,* Brando and Cox zoomed around on their motorcycles in identical white T-shirts and jeans, stubbles of beard on their chins. Wally, the skinny, bespectacled guy, "pipsqueak as biker punk," reveled in the irony of his image next to Brando's. Wally called Brando "Marlon Brando the actor," as if he might be confused with Marlon Brando the butcher. Brando called Wally the Walrus because he seemed so serious and intent. Cox had cards made up with "Walrus" and his phone number printed on them.

"They acted like children together, but they also acted like each other's parent," a friend says. "They were very tender with each other."

At parties Wally would get up and do funny monologues about an old school friend named Dufus who would do anything for a laugh. He also did a hilarious takeoff of a noncommissioned officer lecturing recruits. Brando thought his friend's strange, high-pitched ramblings were side-splitting. With his encouragement, Wally got a booking at the nightclub the Village Vanguard. On opening night, when the audience refused to settle down, Brando stood up and roared, "Keep quiet!" Everybody instantly obeyed, and Wally performed his one-man show and got a standing ovation.

In the summer of 1949, after playing his last performance of *Streetcar*—his five hundredth—Brando left immediately for France. He was supposedly going to Paris to meet with French director Claude Autant-Lara to discuss the possibility of starring in the film version of Stendhal's *The Red and the Black*, but it never worked out, so Brando just relaxed.

He holed up in a fleabag hotel and spent part of his time wandering around museums and the Left Bank and drinking in the beauty of the city. He loved being anonymous again. Celia Webb was in Paris; he saw her, and he visited his friend Ellen Adler, who was living in a lovely apartment off the Quai Voltaire with the musician David Oppenheim, whom she ultimately married. Brando also met the director Jean Cocteau and the writer James Baldwin, who introduced him to the novelist Richard Wright.

He spent a great deal of time with the handsome, fun-loving actor Christian Marquand, who became one of his most intimate friends. Marquand knew nothing of Brando's huge success on Broadway. He knew nothing about Brando, period, except that they liked each other enormously. "It was instant rapport," Marquand said. Late one night in a café Brando suddenly began acting out the entire three acts of *Streetcar* for him, playing all the parts. Roger Vadim and his new wife, Brigitte Bardot, were there too. "We were all extremely impressed," Vadim recalls.

Near the end of his vacation Brando went off to Italy and spent a few days in Rome. Then he traveled to Naples. Having driven into the countryside, he "lay down in a field of flowers and fell asleep, lulled by the Mediterranean sun." When he woke up, he stared up at the clear blue cloudless sky, and he experienced—he later told a reporter—"the only moment of pure happiness" he had ever known.

When he returned to New York, he discovered that a couple of his friends had sneaked into his apartment (Wally was off somewhere working) and had stolen everything in sight: books, records, clothes. The place was wiped clean. In those early years Brando still trusted people and was extremely generous with his money and his home. His door was never locked. He didn't care about possessions; he traveled with only two pairs of jeans and a couple of T-shirts.

Still, he was surprised to wake up that morning after he came back from Paris and find yet another "friend" rifling through the little box on the floor where he kept extra cash. The friend noticed Brando gazing at him silently from the bed. He didn't seem to be the least bit embarrassed. "Hi," the friend said nonchalantly, and gave him what Brando described later as "the look of a jackal."

Time passed, and as Brando became increasingly rich and celebrated, he grew suspicious of certain friends, especially "the hangers-on, the poor ones, the unsuccessful ones," Phil Rhodes says. He got paranoid, believing they were using him for his money, his fame, or his status. "You can't blame him," Pat Cox says, "because Marlon *was* used by a great many people for a long, long time. Wally warned him about that, but he kept ignoring it."

5

IN LATE 1949 BRANDO SIGNED to do his first movie, *The Men,* produced by Stanley Kramer and directed by Fred Zinnemann, with a script by Carl Foreman. Based on much research, it was inspired by a story about a soldier named Ken Wilocek, whose spine had been shattered by a German sniper at the end of the war. Paralyzed from the waist down, he has to struggle to be a man despite this handicap. The paralysis could also be seen as symbolic of the general powerlessness felt in America during the repressive 1950s, with its blacklists and emphasis on conformity.

Brando didn't relate to the symbolism; he related to the story, because to the outside world, little was known about these poor, shattered young men who lay in veterans' hospitals all over the country, marriages broken, fiancées gone, returning to former careers out of the question. How to find a purpose, a reason to go on: This was a dramatic predicament that appealed to Brando. He felt that the story and the character had social significance.

When he arrived in California, he was met by his new

agent, twenty-one-year-old Jay Kanter, who'd just been hired by MCA. They became close friends, and eventually Kanter became his most trusted adviser and one of the few people Brando liked in Hollywood. He hated almost everything about the film community, especially the glaring sun and the nosy gossip columnists who kept at him with inane questions. He was privately worried his face wouldn't photograph well; he briefly considered plastic surgery. He also hated his hands and wondered how they would look on film; even when he was young, they were wrinkled and deeply marked like an old man's.

He was glad to be staying with close family. His aunt, Betty Lindemeyer, put him up in her modest little house in Eagle Rock, a working-class suburb fifteen miles from Hollywood. Nana, his grandmother, was there too. Feisty and good-humored, she raised his spirits briefly. He'd had some bad news from his sister Jocelyn, who had decided to divorce her husband, Don; then he'd heard from Senior, who had experienced severe reversals in a cattle feed scheme he had invested in heavily.

Before he started filming, Brando suddenly began shocking reporters with his rude comments on Hollywood. He called it a frontier town ruled by fear and love of money. "But I'm not afraid of anything and I don't love money," he declared, adding that he'd been born in "outer Mongolia and ate gazelle's eyes for breakfast." When asked about his mother, he retorted, "She's a drunk." As for his background, "It was terrible." Kramer's press agents quickly decided Brando should stop talking to the press for a while.

He wanted to concentrate on researching the role. He asked

to be admitted to the amputees' ward of Birmingham Veterans Hospital in Van Nuys as a paralyzed vet with a background similar to Ken's.

Few members of the staff or patients knew who Brando was, so for a while he was able to blend in with the amputees, a cross section of America: blue-collar workers, farmers, enlisted men. He shared their physiotherapy, spending hours tumbling out of bed and into his wheelchair. He watched the paraplegics reach for their hand exercisers, and so did he. He learned to lift himself out of bed using only his arms. Eventually he was racing down the hall with the amputees in their wheelchairs.

By the end of the third week in the hospital, Brando had been completely accepted by the vets, some of whom played roles in *The Men*. He told them why he was there: He was going to act in a movie about them, and he just wanted to do it right. The vets began confiding in Brando. They told him that they were disappointments to their wives because they would never be able to make love again. Brando became especially close to one vet who had struggled for a year to learn how to light a cigarette, since he no longer had the use of his arms. (Later this man committed suicide.)

At night Brando accompanied the vets to the Pump Room, a popular bar in the San Fernando Valley where they all went to drink. Drink was their only solace. Like the vets, Brando was in a wheelchair, lined up with the others, ordering beer and talking and joking. Once a little old lady, slightly tipsy, staggered over to them and began ranting about the healing powers of Jesus and how if they kept on believing, they might really walk again.

Brando studied her for a long time, and then with a gigantic effort, he hoisted himself up. A few people gasped, and the room fell silent as he took a few halting steps unaided. Everyone else lounging at the bar assumed he was a paraplegic, and waiters stood by to catch him if he fell. The woman stared at him bug-eyed when he burst out laughing and began to perform a softshoe dance up and down the length of the barroom floor before crying out, "I can walk! I can walk!" to the wild applause of the vets as he disappeared into the night.

On the set, things were not as enjoyable. Brando was having difficulty adjusting to moviemaking. He couldn't remember his lines. He hated doing scenes out of sequence, and he was unable to relax as the crew moved about adjusting lights and cables. "He seemed under a huge strain," Zinnemann recalled later. "And he was very defensive. I phoned Kazan, and he assured me, 'Marlon will be all right, just be patient. He'll come through, I promise you.'"

And he did, although for a while he struggled. He felt exhausted by having to turn his feelings on and off. In *The Men* he had a big emotional scene in which he had to acknowledge his sexual impotence to his fiancée. He arrived at the studio at 7:30 A.M. and hid out in his dressing room, loaded with mood music and poetry, anything that would trigger a big emotional response. He played the scene over and over in his mind, rehearsed until he felt moved. But when he walked out in front of the camera at 9:30 A.M., he had nothing left inside himself.

That evening he watched the rushes and thought his performance was terrible, wooden. He never forgot that moment and from then on proceeded to learn how to pace himself on the set so that he wouldn't dry up.

Under Zinnemann's austere and expert direction, Brando not only mastered the mechanics of film acting during the shooting of *The Men* but came through with a heartrending portrayal of someone who faces his limitations and marries his girl; even though he's no longer "whole," he finds purpose and reason to live. "Do you want me to help you up the steps?" asks his new wife, played by the luminous Teresa Wright, and he answers, "Please." He cannot make it alone, but admitting failure doesn't mean he's less manly. Brando was able to express this. In that moment he transcends the traditional macho John Wayne/Clark Gable male screen star image.

The most important thing about this picture, however, is that it was Brando's screen debut, and it has to be considered in relation to the stage work that preceded it and to what followed on film. It is the young Brando, utterly original, true to himself and the character. More than any other actor at that time, Brando presented the ordinary American guy to the public. The interest he engendered, and the acclaim, were a response to the vulnerability he projected as well as the strength. And always his own anger and passion transcend the roles.

The Men did not make Brando a star in Hollywood the way *Streetcar* had made him a star on Broadway, although his reviews were superlative. *Time* magazine: "Broadway's Marlon Brando in his first movie does a magnificent job. His halting, mumbled delivery, glowering silences and expert simulation of paraplegia do not suggest acting; they look chillingly like the real thing."

And the *New York Times*'s Bosley Crowther: "His face, the whole rhythm of his body and especially the strange timbre of his voice, often broken and plaintive... are articulate in every way. Out of stiff and frozen silences he can lash into a passionate rage, with the fearful and flailing frenzy of a taut cable suddenly cut."

However, the movie had the bad fortune to open in July 1950, two weeks after the Korean War had started, and nobody wanted to see a movie about paraplegics. *The Men* died at the box office within two weeks.

Months later Brando started filming the movie version of *A Streetcar Named Desire,* and just as there had never been a performance like it onstage, there would be nothing like it on-screen either.

With his movie earnings from *The Men,* he'd bought his parents a larger farm in the little town of Mundelein, outside Libertyville—forty windswept acres of cornfields, a huge barn, and lilac bushes out front. Dodie loved the place, loved her garden, her plants, driving her pickup truck around to AA meetings, and then bringing some of her AA buddies out to the farm for a meal.

Brando often went to Mundelein. He told his mother he was feeling depressed and low; he had to get back to Mittelmann and his psychoanalysis. The anxiety attacks would not go away. Once or twice he'd lain down in the street until one of them passed. Dodie introduced him to a friend who suffered from the same kind of anxiety attack. The friend gave him some Librium. For the next forty years, on and off,

Librium would be Brando's drug of choice, although it never did that much good.

Dodie, knowing her son's deep love of animals, gave him a baby raccoon. He and Wally Cox named the raccoon Russell after a mutual childhood friend, and when he returned to New York and moved with Wally into another apartment across the street from Carnegie Hall, he took the raccoon with him. Brando adored Russell. He kept him for four years, carrying him on the sets of *Streetcar* and Viva Zapata!, even taking him to Chicago when he was promoting *The Men*. At one point he asked a press agent, "Do you know where my raccoon could get laid?"

Russell was Brando's constant companion. He even slept in Brando's bed, at his feet, and when Russell woke up, he would tickle Brando's toes with his paws. The two would chase each other around the apartment, playing and fighting and tickling each other. Russell once took apart a wristwatch. He loved water, and he splashed for hours in the bathtub, which Brando sometimes filled with stones so it would resemble a creek. Russell enjoyed sitting on the windowsill gazing down at West Fifty-seventh Street, and he liked to perch on Brando's shoulder at parties and watch the guests.

6

BRANDO WAS NOT THAT anxious to repeat Stanley in the movies, believing he had dredged up everything he could inside himself for the part. Also, he was concerned, as he was with anything he did, with the integrity of the project. He was afraid, as was Kazan, that Hollywood might compromise the material. He decided he would not make a decision to star in the film until Warner Brothers and Charlie Feldman, who had obtained the rights, resolved the numerous problems with the Production Code.

Indeed, the Breen Office, which enforced industry censorship, was trying to cut the rape scene, but Tennessee Williams wrote an eloquent letter to Joe Breen saying, "The rape of Blanche by Stanley is a pivotal, integral truth in the play, without which the play loses its meaning, which is the ravishment of the tender, the sensitive, the delicate, by the savage and brutal forces of modern society. It is a poetic plea for comprehension." Breen did relent on the rape but removed all profanity from the script and insisted that Stanley must be "punished." At the end of the movie Stella whispers to her baby that she will never live with Stanley again.

Even with this change, the movie remains a superb documentation of a harsh poetic masterpiece, a reminder of a turning point in theatrical history. That was Kazan's intention: "to do it as filmed theater." Briefly he had toyed with the idea of opening up the story to show why Blanche had been thrown out of town, but he soon realized that the addition diluted *Streetcar*'s power, and he returned to Williams's original script. The drama needed to be played out in those two sweltering rooms in the Vieux Carré.

By April 10, 1950, Brando had agreed to do the film, and the details of his *Streetcar* contract became public. He was to receive eighty thousand dollars (double his salary for *The Men*), billing on all screen, marquee, and advertising credits, veto power over wardrobe fittings, makeup tests, press interviews in the first week of production. As in his contract with Kramer, there was no multipicture clause, leaving him free to pick and choose future roles. In late July he flew out to Los Angeles and moved in with Jay Kanter.

Except for Blanche, the Broadway cast remained intact. Brando always felt that the movie version was better than the play mainly because Vivien Leigh had been cast as Blanche. "She was memorably beautiful, one of the great beauties of the screen," Brando said. He had seen her as Scarlett in *Gone With the Wind* when he was a kid and remembered her as bewitching. Kazan had the impression that "Vivien was being devoured by something she was trying unsuccessfully to control," that her own life was now very much like that of Williams's wounded butterfly Blanche. Subject to frequent

Brando and Vivien Leigh take time out between shooting scenes of *Streetcar* to discuss plans for a surprise birthday party for Elia Kazan.

depressions, she had affairs indiscriminately and had begun to shatter mentally.

At their first meeting, she appeared exquisite, dainty, and impeccably groomed. She'd been curious about Brando, so Kazan had arranged a lunch in Jack L. Warner's private dining room. The press was invited as well.

Brando's opening gambit: "Why do you always wear scent?" Leigh replied, "I like to smell nice—don't you?"

Brando answered that he didn't even take baths: "I just throw a gob of spit in the air and run under it."

Leigh laughed, and then she began parrying questions from reporters, crisply telling them to stop calling her Lady Olivier. "Her Ladyship is fucking bored with such formality."

Atmosphere on the set was tense at first between Leigh and Kazan, because her husband, Sir Laurence Olivier, had directed her in the London stage production of *Streetcar*, and she assumed she would simply be re-creating her stage performance. The first days of shooting, she kept saying, "When Larry and I did the production in London—" and Kazan interrupted and told her gently, "But you're not making the film with Larry in London now, Vivien. You're making it here with us," and she would grow agitated. She finally promised that when she went home, she would not run lines with Olivier.

She began listening to Kazan. "She was the hardest-working actress I've ever met," he said later. "She would crawl over glass if it would make her better." She was the first to arrive at the studio and the last to leave in the evening, Anne Edwards writes in her biography of Leigh. "Vivien wanted to let the audience see what Blanche was like when she was seventeen and in love with her young husband. She surrounded herself with props that would inspire her—a dance card, a gift from an admirer, a picture of the family home."

Often when he wasn't in a scene, Brando enjoyed sitting on the sidelines, watching Kazan work with Vivien Leigh. He enjoyed that, he explained, because "creating emotions in an actor is a delicate proposition...and Gadg was always emotionally involved in the process and his instincts were perfect." Once Brando observed him rehearsing a love scene between Karl Malden and Leigh. As they went over the dialogue, the great director silently mouthed the words with them, moved his hands the way they did, mimicked their expressions and gestures. Brando was amazed to see that when they finished the scene, Kazan immediately realized what was missing and had them do it again.

Gradually Kazan reshaped Vivien Leigh's performance until her strained artificial mannerisms were gone, and she was both pitiable and terrifying. Her female frailty was genuine, and she looked like a Dresden shepherdess doll that had been destroyed. When she cries, "I don't want reality, I want magic," you understand exactly what she's talking about.

Kazan did very little directing with Brando. "There was nothing to do," he said. "Marlon was totally submerged in the part of Stanley. What's interesting is you can see him exploring his female qualities, quite mysterious, and even though he played Stanley five hundred times on Broadway, whenever I'd watched him in the rushes it was as if it was happening for the first time. His preparation, his memories, desires were so deep, all I had to do was to help him keep them fresh."

Now there seemed an even greater entrapment between Blanche and Stanley. The themes that Williams was writing about seemed heightened on film: confronting or denying the complex ties and ambiguities of our sexuality, and the costs of either strategy.

Working with Leigh galvanized Brando. "He was genuinely attracted to her and he used it. He hadn't been attracted to Jessie Tandy," Kazan wrote. Maybe that was part of the problem on Broadway, but it was different in the movie. Vivien's wild sexual craziness, her flirtatiousness, her faded southern belle appearance turned him on. Brando exuded a rage and a passion even greater than on the stage. His hostility with Leigh was so raw it was frightening. Her exquisite manners bugged him. "Why are you so fucking polite?" he'd growl at her. During a closeup "I once saw spittle spraying from his lips and onto Vivien's cheeks," Kazan recalled.

"It was almost as if they'd created a magic circle to exist in," critic Molly Haskell wrote of their most passionate scenes together, "not out of reality but out of equal degrees of unreality. They were creatures of absolute fantasy, and Kazan knew instinctively how to deal with them, how to channel the larger-than-life electricity between them so that it was at once mystical and pseudo-real."

As shooting progressed, Brando softened toward Vivien Leigh. Between takes, they'd relax in their chairs, smoking cigarettes, and he would entertain her with silly jokes and funny faces. Sometimes he would make her laugh by doing a devastatingly accurate imitation of her husband, Sir Laurence Olivier, in the famous Agincourt speech from *Henry V*. And sometimes he'd sing her folk songs—"songs my mother taught me," like "Streets of Laredo" and "Don't Fence Me In."

Often she complained of being depleted by Blanche. She told Brando she'd heard voices when she acted *Streetcar* in London. "Blanche is a woman with everything stripped away," she said. "She is a tragic figure and I understand her. But playing her has often tripped me into madness."

Near the end of the shoot Brando realized she was quite ill. Suffering from tuberculosis, she needed to leave the set early, and Olivier was usually waiting in her dressing room to take her home.

When shooting was over, the Oliviers invited Brando to dinner at their rented house in Bel Air, and he went, dressed neatly in a business suit. They told him to take off his tie and relax, and he laughed. "They had had little opportunity to talk to him during the weeks of filming...they found they had much in common," writes Brando biographer Charles Higham. "All three hated pretense, phoniness, the absurdities of Hollywood at its worst...the whole tragic comedy of life itself. It was in every way a wonderful evening and they would never forget it."

While Brando and his fellow actors were filming *Streetcar*, the House Un-American Activities Committee (HUAC) had launched another investigation into alleged Communist subversion in the film industry. The Hollywood studios had already established a blacklist, and many writers, actors, and directors who were refusing to cooperate with HUAC by "naming names" of alleged Communists were seeing their careers destroyed.

Brando had no idea that Kazan was worried, that it would

be only a matter of time before he would be called upon to testify to his political beliefs. Once he told Brando that he had been a member of the Communist party, very briefly, in the 1930s. He and Clifford Odets both had belonged to a cell that met in the basement of the Belasco Theater.

Brando had been dabbling in left-wing politics ever since he'd championed the Irgun (the Jewish underground) during the run of *A Flag Is Born*. While he was in *Streetcar,* he worked for Henry Wallace's presidential campaign in 1948, even signing autographs "Vote for Wallace—Marlon Brando." He'd asked Kazan if he was going to vote for Wallace, who was backed by the Communist party, but Kazan wouldn't say. In 1949, Brando and Jocelyn attended the widely criticized World Peace Conference at the Waldorf-Astoria, joining notables like Lillian Hellman and Norman Mailer, but Kazan had not attended. Kazan was keeping a low profile, and in Hollywood he kept a low profile too, refusing to go to the tempestuous meeting of the Screen Directors Guild at which the membership voted in open ballot to adopt a loyalty oath. Instead he completed cutting and editing *Streetcar*. It was granted a Production Code seal, but its censorship problems weren't over.

The film was booked to play in Radio City Music Hall in the spring of 1951, but it was withdrawn because the Legion of Decency had threatened to place it on its condemned list, making it a sin for Catholics to see the film. Without Kazan's consent and by order of Jack Warner, cuts were made to stress Stella's goodness and Stanley's cruelty. In the sequence in which Stella descends the stairs after her fight with Stanley, her close-up and Alex North's sensuous jazz background music were removed; they were considered "too carnal." Kazan was incensed, but there was nothing he could do about it. He wrote a letter to the *New York Times,* explaining what had happened.

Finally *Streetcar* was released that September. It was a huge critical success, winning the New York Film Critics Award and Screen Writers Guild Award. *Time* and Cue magazines put it on their best movies lists, and Bosley Crowther called it the best film of the year; Brando's performance was praised as extraordinary. The film was nominated for twelve Oscars, and Leigh, Hunter, and Malden all won Academy Awards at the ceremonies in 1952. But Kazan was overlooked, he was sure, because he was so hot politically. By then he'd given secret testimony on where his loyalty lay, and his testimony had been leaked to the *Hollywood Reporter.* Brando was overlooked too, although he had probably given one of the most revolutionary performances in the history of cinema.

However, the industry was running scared, with the blacklists, censorship, and the Supreme Court ruling that the studios could no longer simultaneously produce, exhibit, and distribute movies—not to mention the growing popularity of television. To the industry, Brando symbolized the future, and he was barbarous, mumbling, unknown. It wasn't his grungy lifestyle or that he'd emerged from Broadway and the intellectual left-wing theatrical traditions of Stella Adler and the Actors Studio. What really rankled Hollywood was the utter contempt in which Brando seemed to hold the entire film community.

By now stories about his behavior were legendary: how he preferred only women of color; how he'd driven down

Hollywood Boulevard with a fake arrow stuck through his forehead. He refused to bow down to the most powerful gossip columnists in the country, openly referring to Louella Parsons as "the fat one" and Hedda Hopper as "the one with the hat." Then there was his description of personal interviews: He characterized them as "navel picking AND SMOKING IT!"

So why did Hollywood put up with him? His dazzling performance in *Streetcar* but, beyond that, his presence. "The character of Stanley fucked them all," said actor Anthony Quinn. "The whole thing up until then, everything was proper. Robert Taylor, Tyrone Power, Van Johnson, and along comes Brando. It was the character, his Napoleonic Code speech—'A man is a king, by the fucking Constitution, he's a king.' That statement turned the whole world around."

As for Brando, he'd already retreated to New York and gone back to the New School to study French. But he'd decided he would never again return to the Broadway stage. Years later he said, "It's been said I sold out. Maybe that's true—but I knew what I was doing. I've never had any respect for Hollywood. It stands for greed, avarice, phoniness, crass-ness—but when you act in a movie, you act for three months and then you can do what you want for the rest of the year."

7

A YEAR WENT BY BETWEEN the filming of *The Men* and *Streetcar*. Brando continued to live as he always had. He stayed at his apartment on West Fifty-seventh Street with his raccoon and with Wally Cox, who soon became famous as TV's Mr. Peepers, an oddball biology teacher given to saying things like "Class, who can give examples of how ornithology is helpful in the real estate business?"

Back at the apartment, the hangers-on, the losers, and the trash were still congregating around him, Pat Cox recalled. "Marlon was paying for hospital bills, for abortions, and there were a lot of plain handouts. Wally had told him to stop, but for a long time Marlon wouldn't because he felt best when he was helping someone."

By the spring of 1951 Senior had told his son he needed shelters to reduce income taxes, so Brando handed over virtually all his money to his father to invest in a big cattle ranch in the sand hills of Nebraska. Soon Senior and Dodie lived on the ranch full-time, and they gave the farm in Illinois to

Frannie and her husband, Dick Loving. Meanwhile Brando was mastering French, Italian, and Spanish at the New School. He saw the Adlers and Dr. Mittelmann. His anxiety and depressions continued.

On the set of *Streetcar,* Kazan had come to him with a rough draft of a script by the novelist John Steinbeck. It was about Emiliano Zapata, a legendary Mexican revolutionary who stopped at nothing, including murder and arson, to lead his people to freedom during the Mexican civil war of 1910. Then he was assassinated by the very troops he'd commanded and by the very government he'd helped found.

Film scholars have since maintained that this movie mirrored Kazan's obsession with the themes of betrayal and informing. The director often told Brando that Zapata had intrigued him because he was a character who, after he got power, walked away from it. However, Kazan and Steinbeck, both ex-Communists, had wanted to show metaphorically how the Stalinsts fared in the Soviet Union after the revolution: how their leaders turned reactionary and repressive. This movie gave Kazan the chance to attack Stalinism.

Brando ignored the metaphors in the script. What appealed to him was the story of an orphaned peasant, earthy and primitive, who fights passionately for justice. (Even in the repressive 1950s Brando's films connect maleness with social rebellion.)

In the next month he went off to Sonora, Mexico, to soak up atmosphere. He enjoyed living with the peasants, interviewing old people who had actually known Zapata. Legend has it that Zapata had carried out more than a thousand executions and had twenty wives.

Brando studied photographs of Zapata, whose fierce, lean face bore no resemblance to his own rather soft, dreamy countenance. The movie makeup that transformed him was done by Phil Rhodes, who became one of his closest friends. Rhodes was a kind of Renaissance man with a law degree and an extensive background in philosophy, literature, and art. When he and Brando first met in New York in 1947, he was an actor and a model and was already earning money doing makeup and facial sculpting, something Brando was fascinated with. Rhodes's expertise in makeup was to play a crucial part in shaping the visual impact of most of Brando's performances. For Zapata, the two men experimented with rubber latex masks that pushed Brando's eyelids up, and he wore a two-way stretch plate inside his mouth, a jet-black wig, and a mustache, until he was transformed into an Indian.

Brando tried to perfect a Spanish accent, the only member of the cast who did, and he was annoyed in retrospect when he heard himself on-screen because he thought he sounded artificial. Kazan had cast supporting roles from the Actors Studio, and everyone else in the picture sounded as if he'd been born in Brooklyn.

In Mexico, Brando met a black-haired actress, thirty-three-year-old Movita Castenada (who as a teenager had played opposite Clark Gable in the original *Mutiny on the Bounty*). Marlon "was absolutely smitten with her," Phil Rhodes said. "She reminded him of a Gypsy, a primitive, and she believed everything he told her." Brando got her a job as an extra in *Zapata* so he could take her with him on location. They remained together off and on for the next fifteen years; she was the most important of his many women. "She was a stabilizing influence," Sondra Lee says, "a mother figure." She eventually became Brando's second wife.

The ten-week shoot was in Roma, Texas. The production wasn't allowed to film in Mexico because the Mexican government thought the film was too left-wing and it didn't approve of the mostly non-Hispanic actors. Jean Peters, who later married Howard Hughes, had been cast as Zapata's wife, Josefa, and Joseph Wiseman played the journalist Fernando, who betrays Zapata. Wiseman gives the most eccentric performance in the film—he is hypermanic, in direct contrast with Brando's brooding peasant—but it is Fernando's speeches that contain much of what Kazan and Steinbeck wanted to say politically.

Anthony Quinn, half Mexican, half Irish, a boisterous boxer and painter, was the brother of Brando's Zapata in the film. Quinn had replaced Brando in *Streetcar*, and Harold Clurman, who'd directed him, thought that although Brando was the better actor, Quinn had served the play better. Uta Hagen, who played Blanche with both actors, said, "Marlon was too sensitive for Stanley. Tony Quinn *was* better because he's a brute. But he doesn't know he's a brute."

It was very hot in Roma, 120 degrees in the shade. Kazan often directed bare-chested. All the actors sweated profusely, and he thought "the heat did something to their faces. They lost their actorish look."

When he wasn't filming, Brando spent his free time by himself, either in his trailer or wandering around the countryside, usually in costume and makeup, with his raccoon, Russell, on a leash. Sometimes he'd feed him milk shakes, and the raccoon would hold the drink in his tiny paws and slurp it down in one gulp. In the evenings Brando would set off fireworks outside the local hotel to relax, and later he and Kazan would swim naked in the Rio Grande.

The director was delighting in Brando's performance. With Zapata, he was playing a peasant in another place, another time. It was totally invented. "I told him," said Kazan, "'a peasant does not reveal what he thinks. Things happen to him and he shows no reaction.' He has a peasant's watchful wariness, the illiterate sense that words can entrap."

Kazan told him, "Zapata doesn't romanticize women. That was easy for Marlon to understand, because he didn't romanticize women either, except maybe his mother." Kazan watched women come on to Brando all the time. "They were all available to Marlon, but I rarely saw him respond. His warmest relations were with the men."

With the exception of Tony Quinn. Quinn was irritated because Kazan seemed to be paying more attention to Brando, giving him all the close-ups, coddling him: Are you okay? Did you sleep well? Was the heat too much? "Okay, okay, it was like he was his son!" Quinn complained.

Kazan tried to get the two actors to be friends. After all, they were playing brothers. "Talk to each other, you guys," he'd say. "But we couldn't think of anything to talk about," Quinn recalls. One day Brando suggested they take a stroll over to some cactus plants. Quinn didn't want to but finally sauntered after him. "And we got there and Marlon began pissing and suggested I do the same. 'At least we can relieve ourselves together,' he said." For a while the two had pissing contests: Who could piss farthest?

Finally came the climactic scene in the movie, the fight between the two Zapata brothers, a scene that culminates in a gigantic outburst. Brando writes about the scene in his autobiography, describing how Kazan told "Tony some lies about what I'd said behind his back." And Kazan did the same thing to Brando, implying Quinn was bragging to everybody about how much better he had been in *Streetcar* than Brando. It brought out what Kazan had wanted: a killing rage between the two actors. So the fight between them is vicious. In it, Brando seems to have lost control. He even yanks at Quinn's hair. Quinn said later, "I wanted to stick my sword in him."

Kazan never told Quinn he'd made up Brando's remarks, nor did he tell Brando what he'd done. He loved to create off-camera dramas that would mimic and enhance what he wanted to see on camera. After they shot the scene, the two actors didn't speak for fifteen years. And then one evening Brando heard Quinn on a TV talk show describe what had happened on *Zapata*. As soon as the show was over, Brando phoned him to explain that "Gadg had been manipulating both of us for the good of the movie. It was a relief to clear up that incident. From then on, Tony and I started speaking. Gadg inspired a lot of actors, but you paid a price."

What makes this movie important for Brando as an actor is that he was now, after three movies, totally in control in front of the camera. He could ignore the technical aspects of moviemaking and concentrate on acting and trusting his instincts, which he did in this film, and he gives us a portrait of a revolutionary in despair and defeat and confusion. There's an added dimension to his screen persona, too, that was missing from *The Men* and Streetcar: Now Brando is the crusader riding a white horse across the dusty hills—an image of male as liberator.

Viva Zapata! opened in February 1952. It was a big success, and Brando got rave reviews. He was nominated for his second Oscar as Zapata, but Quinn won best supporting Oscar for his role as Zapata's brother.

So far Brando had played a peasant and a brute. He was now identified in the public's mind as a crude, ill-mannered slob. So when it was announced that in his next movie he would play Marc Antony in Shakespeare's *Julius Caesar*, gossip columnists like Hedda Hopper sneered and TV comics such as Jerry Lewis and Sid Caesar did devastating impersonations of Stanley Kowalski delivering the famous "Friends, Romans, countrymen" speech. *Collier's* magazine described Brando as "The Neanderthal Man."

"I'm sick to death of being thought of as a blue-jeaned slobbermouth," Brando complained. Privately he was terrified of working with the likes of John Gielgud, James Mason, and Deborah Kerr, some of the cast that director Joseph Mankiewicz had assembled in Hollywood. Brando's mother urged him to do Shakespeare. So he went back to the farm and worked with her on the role for a week, shouting the lines "Friends, Romans, countrymen!" in one of the cornfields until he lost his voice.

Later, in the spring of 1952, he took off for Paris to relax and spend time with friends, including Christian Marquand. He'd been there only a few days when he ran into playwright

Arthur Laurents, later one of the authors of *West Side Story*. He was waving a copy of the *Herald Tribune* and crying out, "Gadg has informed!"

According to the news story in the *Trib*, Kazan had gone in front of the House Un-American Activities Committee and had named eight of his friends from the Group Theatre, including Paula Strasberg and the playwright Clifford Odets.

Brando knew that in February Kazan had given secret testimony to the committee in which he had answered all its questions, including the fact that he had once been a Communist, but he had refused to name names. Now he had suddenly gone back on his word and betrayed his friends. This action went against everything Brando believed Kazan stood for. The plays he'd directed on Broadway, like *Death of a Salesman* and *All My Sons*, contained themes of conscience and personal honor. And his movies too had social significance: *Gentleman's Agreement* dealt with anti-Semitism, and *Viva Zapata!* was about the importance of revolution. Kazan had been like a father to Brando, and their collaborations had been crucial to his development as an actor.

Returning to New York, he dropped by the Actors Studio and discovered that the membership was up in arms. Kazan was the most powerful director in the country. Everyone felt he could have used his clout to fight the blacklist and fight the committee, but he had caved in.

After Mae Reis, Kazan's secretary, quit in protest, the members called a meeting to decide how to deal with the situation. Kazan's position was that he had never judged *them* politically, why should they judge *him*? Ultimately the Actors

Studio chose to remain apolitical, but Kazan did not return there for a long time, and by the time he did, Lee Strasberg had assumed the role of master teacher.

Meanwhile the naming of names as a test of virtue determined and defined the Cold War environment. In the next months Clifford Odets was to inform, and so did Jerome Robbins and Lee J. Cobb. The actor John Garfield died unexpectedly. He'd been pressured to name names but refused, and everyone said the pressure had killed him. Brando had dinner at the Adlers' and listened to Harold Clurman mournfully speak about the social consequences of Gadg's "failure of spirit."

For his part, Brando made no move to see Kazan, but he remained preoccupied by his betrayal. He had begun work on *Julius Caesar,* and its director, Joe Mankiewicz, remembers that during a rehearsal break Brando suddenly started crying. "What'll I do when I see him? Bust him in the nose?" Mankiewicz tried to tell him that Kazan was in pain too. That didn't seem to help Brando's anguish.

He threw himself into his work, spending hours with a voice coach, listening to recordings of every great Shakespearean actor from John Gielgud and John Barrymore to Laurence Olivier. He periodically called his mother for encouragement, and she would tell him he would be magnificent. She hated his reputation as mumblemouth.

Mankiewicz recalled filming a scene in which Brando, as Marc Antony, realizes he will replace Caesar. He finds himself alone in an outdoor garden filled with ruined statues and a huge bust of the murdered emperor. Slowly, without any directorial prompting. Brando turned the bust so it gazed directly at him. Outside, a mob is burning Rome. "And you saw Marlon transform himself into that statue. He had found his visual key," Mankiewicz told a gathering at the Actors Studio years later. "There was this great actor, standing amidst those marble figures in their sculpted drapery, and there was such simplicity and balance in that image because it so totally contained his silence. One closeup of that look of Brando's— it was like a piece of exquisite music."

When *Julius Caesar* opened in New York on May 8, 1953, Brando was a revelation to everybody. Bosley Crowther of the *Times* said, "Happily, Mr. Brando's diction, which has been guttural and slurred in previous films, is clear and precise in this instance....A major talent emerges." And the *Sydney Morning Herald* added, "Brando's speeches over the dead Caesar are a magnificent mixture of grief and self-steadying diplomacy; and the great Roman oration is shot with new feelings."

That was because Brando had asked Gielgud to record it for him and also to give him notes, as he did, and Brando incorporated all his suggestions, so "it had wonderful color and pacing," the great English actor said. Afterward he invited Brando to costar with Paul Scofield in a classical season he was planning to direct at Hammersmith, but Brando said he didn't want to act in the theater again.

Brando went on to win another Academy Award nomination for *Julius Caesar*, his third in three years, but he didn't care. What mattered was that he had proved he could do the classics, and his mother thought he was indeed nothing short of magnificent.

He was now Hollywood's most talked-about and in-demand star. He turned down script after script, including *East of Eden,* which Kazan originally asked him to do. Instead James Dean won the part of Steinbeck's tortured antihero and gave a remarkable performance of physical and vocal intensity.

At Actors Studio parties, Brando would run into Dean, who eventually symbolized the "misunderstood, hotrodding American youth with a switchblade approach to life's little problems," Truman Capote wrote. At the moment Dean had a reputation as "someone who was driven by demons." A slender farm boy from Indiana who also had a terrible relationship with his father, Dean worshiped Brando and copied everything about him: his slouch, his jeans, his loaded silences and sullen expression. He learned to play the drums and ride a motorcycle. They even dated the same woman, Ursula Andress, for a while.

"Dean used to call me," Brando said. "I'd listen to him talking into my answering machine, asking for me, leaving messages, but I never spoke up."

At one party he watched Dean acting like a wild man, even mimicking his own fractured mumble, and he tried to set Dean straight. "*Be yourself,*" he told him sternly. With that, Dean let loose with his strange high-pitched giggle. Brando then suggested that he see an analyst, and he gave him Bela Mittelmann's phone number.

8

BY 1953 BRANDO HAD MADE four movies. He was indisputably famous. He hated being famous and bothered by fans, who followed him down the street and into movie theaters and even into the corner deli, asking for his autograph and calling out, "Marlon!" Some were more aggressive, like the trio of girls who camped on his doorstep and refused to leave, or the female stalker who papered her apartment with *Streetcar* posters and threatened to kidnap him.

Life was easier in Los Angeles because the sidewalks were empty—everybody was in a car—and he could hop on his motorcycle and zoom off into the desert, sometimes with a girl and sometimes not. He would ride and ride, hoping he might run out of gas and die in the sun.

Back in New York, he'd occasionally go to parties at Norman Mailer's loft on Monroe Street because people didn't bother him there, and the place reminded him of his own apartment. It was like a dark cave with manuscripts scattered around and records and jazz playing and people swarming about in the various rooms.

Usually the original Beat contingent made an appearance: the poet Allen Ginsberg, the writers William Burroughs and Jack Kerouac. They all had secret crushes on Brando, but they never made any moves; they just looked at him soulfully. They were on "spiritual journeys." That's what "Beat" meant, Kerouac would say. "Beat, beatific": trying to find out the meaning of life. Everybody was reading Wilhelm Reich's *The Function of the Orgasm.* Its thesis: A lot of sex cures all psychosomatic ailments.

Norman Mailer, hugely famous after the success of his first novel, *The Naked and the Dead,* was the center of attention at his parties, often high on marijuana and speaking in various accents—Brooklyn, Irish, a Texas drawl. Like Brando, he felt "prominent and empty." He believed his celebrity had a power not linked to anything he felt. "At the time, I used to complain that everything seemed unreal," Mailer said. "It took me years to realize that my experience was the only one I would have to remember."

The two men had an uneasy relationship. Once at a big Hollywood gathering they had a little confrontation. Brando demanded, "Shouldn't you be home writing, Norman?" Mailer later called Brando "our noblest actor and our national lout."

Back in the 1950s, at these parties, Brando kept a distance from all the other guests and rarely said a word. Celia Webb might be on his lap, smoking cigarette after cigarette. Once George Plimpton arrived in black tie and tux via the fire escape. Another time, very late, a group of punks burst in

Brando in *The Wild One*, the movie that gave him legendary status. It's pure Brando – sweaty sexuality and a mumbling, hostile attitude, combined with a prizefighter's body and a poet's face.

and inexplicably hit Mailer with a hammer. It was Montgomery Clift who rushed to Mailer's aid while Brando remained on the couch watching.

He'd been turning down every script he was offered. Then Stanley Kramer came to him with the idea for a movie that he liked, *The Wild One*, based on a magazine article about a band of rowdy motorcyclists wrecking a small town in Northern California, terrorizing and enraging its citizens. The focus would be on youthful rebels in search of excitement, anything to contain their huge unchanneled energy.

Kramer thought this would dramatize the tensions that were arising between the generations in the 1950s. American society had never been so prosperous or so uninspired and uniform, and as a result, adolescents were becoming like aliens. It could be a study of violence versus authority, Kramer said. Brando would play the biker gang leader. He was intrigued by the concept of alienated youth, since he saw himself as alienated. He could draw on his own hostility to convention.

The movie was shot in twenty-four days on the back lot of Columbia Pictures in Hollywood. Columbia's president, Harry Cohn, hated the project and wanted to spend as little money as possible on it. The Breen Office had already come down on the original script as "Communist" because in it the bikers had seemed sympathetic in the censors' eyes. The original screenplay had implied that all was not right in a society that could produce such violent rebels. During the 1950s there was no political rebellion, just repression. The kids seemed to be the only ones who were angry about the overriding apathy.

The revised script was terrible. In essence, it said that the bike raid was a one-time happening and couldn't happen again. But for Brando the whole point was it *could* happen again. He told Kramer he felt that he'd sold out, but he was going to go ahead with the project anyway.

Brando tried his hand at rewrites, but it did no good, so he ended up simply ad-libbing and improvising entire scenes, halting and tense, with some pretty memorable results, as in the first scene in the café, where he orders coffee from the pretty waitress (the love interest) and starts to flirt. No more than a couple of minutes on the screen, and he is funny and touching and unconsciously sexy. All he does is lazily push a quarter back and forth across the counter. The waitress tries to grab it, and he slides it away from her. It's like a cat playing with a mouse. The waitress is totally flummoxed and charmed and attracted in spite of herself. Then she starts asking questions. "What do your gang members do? Do you go on a picnic or something?"

Brando answers, "A picnic, man! You're too square. You just go...the idea is to have a ball. Now if you stay cool, you gotta wail." This is all Brando, drawing from conversations he'd had with a real motorcycle gang he'd hung out with in Hollister. It's a combination of their lingo and jazz expressions, all spoken, Norman Mailer says, "in the soft insinuating animal voice of the hipster."

The café was also the setting for the famous exchange that was to be another 1950s emblem. The waitress asks plaintively, "Johnny, what are you rebelling against?" and Brando replies, "Whaddaya got?"

"I don't get you at all," a cop says after the biker gang and the townspeople have had various outbursts. "I don't think you know what you want or how to go about it." Brando just sits there, filling the silence. What he doesn't say is more powerful than if he spoke.

His inarticulate eloquence provides the most insightful moments in a movie that is otherwise pretty inconclusive. The fight between rival gang leader Lee Marvin and Brando is tame; the only sinister moment is when the bikers circle the waitress, and that has considerable power.

The film concludes with Johnny's being mistaken for a rapist. He is almost lynched, then savagely beaten by terrified citizens turned vigilantes. Critics have pointed out this is the first of many ritual beatings Brando endures in the movies for playing outsiders and nonconformists.

The Wild One was a failure when it came out; almost everyone took off on the violence. The movie was banned in Britain for ten years, and Brando was devastated. "We started out doing something worthwhile, exploring the psychology of the hipster, trying to show why young people often resort to violence out of frustration," he said, "but instead all we showed was the violence." He really disliked the movie and added to friends, "My ass was too fat." He'd started gorging on food during filming, he was so unhappy with the way the movie was being done.

No one was more surprised than he at the film's ultimate impact: at the thousands of T-shirts and leather jackets and blue jeans sold. These outfits became symbols of rebellion, and *The Wild One* gave Brando legendary status. Everything seemed to come together for him in that film; it is pure Brando. The sweaty sexuality, the mumbling, hostile attitude, combined with his prizefighter's chunky body and his poet's face: That contradiction would remain Brando's fascination to an audience. He was our questing, restless spirit, our original rebel without a cause, always linked to lower-class anti-hero characters, despite his efforts to have a career in which he could assert his versatility.

His myth lived on into the 1960s. Tom Hayden, a California state senator till 2001, says that while he was at Northwestern and helped lead Students for a Democratic Society, which influenced much of the 1960s social and political upheaval, one image kept flashing through his mind: Brando in the movie *The Wild One.* Hayden kept hearing that memorable, all-embracing question "What are you rebelling against?" and Brando's answer: "Whaddaya got?"

Brando hated being thought of as a myth. "But I've learned that no matter what I say or do, people mythologize me," he writes. He would write letters to fans telling them he was just like one of several billion other human animals who are happy and sad. "The greatest change that success has brought me," he went on, "has nothing to do with my concept of myself or my reaction to fame, but of *other* people's reactions to it. I haven't changed. I have never forgotten my life in Libertyville when I felt unwanted."

He had planned to go on to Europe after *The Wild One,* but when he returned to New York, he decided instead to organize a summer stock tour of George Bernard Shaw's *Arms and the Man,* and he cast it with some of his friends like Janice Mars and Billy Redfield. Maureen Stapleton and Wally Cox tagged along too. The Brando name got the tour booked in little theaters all over the eastern seaboard. "It was a wild summer," Mars recalls.

Tammy Grimes, then fifteen and an apprentice at Falmouth Playhouse on Cape Cod, says that Brando "was absolutely mesmerizing onstage, even when he was improvising hilarious monologues of double talk." He hadn't bothered to memorize all his lines. Some of the audience didn't appreciate that; critics panned the show. But everyone had a good time, especially Brando, who wrote his parents he was not "ruffled" by his dissenters. In August he went off to Europe with Billy Redfield; they visited Christian Marquand in Paris and then traveled to the south of France.

When Brando came back to his West Fifty-seventh Street apartment in New York, he discovered that his pet raccoon, Russell, had matured and become uncontrollable. He'd "peed on every record I owned, and the apartment looked as though it had been through a drug raid." Although he didn't want to, Brando took his beloved pet back to the family farm in Mundelein and left him in the barn snuggled in a big bed of hay. "I had a lump in my throat," he writes. "I miss him."

9

BY 1953 ALL BRANDO NEEDED to confirm his status as the greatest actor of his generation was a role that would highlight his ability to convey the paradoxical meanings in a character. That role would be Terry Malloy, the punch-drunk ex-fighter in *On the Waterfront* who turns heroic when he informs on his corrupt union bosses. Brando turned the part down because Elia Kazan would be the director, and he remained conflicted about Gadg's testimony before HUAC, so Frank Sinatra was cast as Terry.

Months went by. Finally, pressured by his agent, Jay Kanter, and by the producer, Sam Spiegel (who always wanted Brando and who argued, "Politics has nothing to do with this—it's about your talent, it's about your career"), Brando read the *Waterfront* script. He decided he should play Terry since he related to "a guy who was driven crazy by his inner conflicts" and also because "Gadg is good for me [as an actor]."

However, he had one condition: He would do *Waterfront* only if he could leave location every afternoon at four to keep his appointment with his psychiatrist, Bela Mittelmann. Spiegel didn't put up any argument.

Before rehearsals started, Kazan and Brando met privately in the director's office. The loyal Karl Malden (who never made any judgment on Kazan's politics) was helping with the *Waterfront* casting; he watched as the two men went into the back room and shut the door.

That day Kazan told Brando that *On the Waterfront* (written by Budd Schulberg and based on a series of articles about mob control of the docks) was about the necessity of speaking out in certain circumstances; that sometimes it is harmful to keep quiet; and that Terry, in testifying against the mobsters on the docks, was doing a noble thing. He admitted there were some parallels to what he had done in front of HUAC. He, Kazan, had informed to break open the secrecy of the Communist party. He had no regrets, and he was quite defiant. He insisted he had not done it for money. Brando writes in his autobiography, "What I didn't realize then was that *On the Waterfront* was really a metaphorical argument by Gadg and Budd Schulberg; they made the film to justify finking on their friends." (Schulberg had also named names and didn't regret it, and this bonded him with Kazan.)

Brando began researching the role of Terry Malloy. He went down to the Hoboken docks and loaded crates the way Terry did and hung around with the workers. Malloy had also been a boxer, and Kazan wanted Brando to move like one, so he had him work out on a daily basis, trading punches at Stillman's Gym and at the Actors Studio with Roger Donoghue, a former light heavyweight. Brando studied Donoghue con-

Brando and Eva Marie Saint in *On the Waterfront*. The two had many scenes together, and the chemistry between them was intense.

stantly and used him as one of his visual models for Terry Malloy.

Sometimes Kazan would say, "I see Terry all by himself in his furnished room, shadowboxing and so blue and alone he's about to cry."

The first read-through of *On the Waterfront* was held at the Actors Studio on November 15, 1953. The entire cast was present: Lee J. Cobb as the corrupt union boss, Karl Malden as the chain-smoking waterfront priest, Rod Steiger as Terry's two-faced older brother, other actors from the studio—Martin Balsam, Leif Erickson, Rudy Bond, Ward Costello—and Brando, of course, chewing gum and looking very serious. Then there was a fragile twenty-one-year-old blond actress named Eva Marie Saint, who'd been cast only two days before as Terry's girl, Edie Doyle, after Kazan decided against using Joanne Woodward. Malden had suggested Eva Saint. He'd worked with her in a scene at the studio and thought she'd be perfect. She'd auditioned for Kazan with Brando. Together they'd done a little improvisation. "Marlon just asked me to dance and then he took me in his arms and we twirled around the floor, and there was so much at stake for me and it was so emotionally powerful, I burst into tears," Saint recalled.

The day-by-day shoot of *Waterfront* was brutal. Temperatures hovered below zero on the frigid Hoboken piers, where most of the movie was shot. There were constant problems with waterfront thugs. The word was out that the script was actually very critical of the Mafia. After a while Kazan hired a bodyguard. Brando, dressed in a greasy plaid jacket and old work pants, took the subway every morning with Saint; he thought if he traveled the tube with a lot of other regular joes, he'd soak up more atmosphere. As soon as they arrived on the docks, they huddled by big bonfires flaring in steel drums, or they escaped into the local hotel, inappropriately named the Grand, for hot coffee.

In the beginning of *Waterfront*, Brando, as Terry Malloy, appears semiconscious, unaware of the struggle that appears to be going on inside him. He doesn't even seem to be listening at first; this is about a man who starts to hear after being psychologically deaf.

"The real action for Terry is an inner one. The drama is internal," Kazan kept saying. "He tries to swagger and appear jaunty, but what betrays him are his eyes." The way Brando uses his eyes in *Waterfront* is the key to his characterization. When Terry realizes he's being used by union bosses to set up the murder of a dockworker, you see him struggling to think for the first time. His sidelong glances and faraway looks signal character confusion as the tug-of-war inside himself between conscience and complacency develops into a full-scale battle. There is a double drama going on between what Terry says and what Terry feels and thinks, and Brando always shows us how the character thinks, without saying a word. You can see the thoughts passing across his face and eyes, and you can hear how "his insides jam up his voice...His furtive looks complement the fractured speech patterns he develops," wrote Foster Hirsch in his detailed study *Acting Hollywood Style*.

Eva Marie Saint remembers how kind Brando was to her. It was her first picture; she was nervous and scared. "Marlon and I would have lunch every day," and when she got cold, he would wrap her up in blankets and give her back rubs, but always in character as Terry. "He *was* Terry," she said. Their relationship on-screen is fragile and physical and truly beautiful to watch. There is intimacy between them because they don't touch until the middle of the movie, when they have that explosive embrace in her bedroom after he has broken down the door to force her to admit she loves him.

The two of them have many memorable scenes together, especially the celebrated glove scene, which started off as an improvisation. Saint says, "In that scene there was no reason for me to talk to him because he was implicated in my brother's murder. And then Marlon suggested, 'Drop your glove,' and I did, and he picked it up and put it on his own hand. If he hadn't done that, I would have walked off, but it was freezing cold, and I wanted my glove back, so we started to talk."

Throughout the movie Brando seemed to work off Saint, and she in turn worked off him. The intensity between them is magnetic. "Marlon was *involved,* which is different from being committed," Kazan said. "Most of it was underneath. His immersion in Terry was complete."

This was most vividly expressed in the justly famous taxicab scene between Rod Steiger and Brando. Peter Manso describes this scene, which was shot on an especially chaotic day. They'd originally planned to film it in traffic, but it proved too time-consuming. Then they discovered that Spiegel had been too cheap to get them a real cab, and they had to improvise in the shell of an old one, on a sound stage, with no rear projection to provide a background. So cinematographer Boris Kaufman hung up some venetian blinds in the back of the cab and shot through them, while two crew members rocked the shell of the cab back and forth to simulate a moving vehicle, and electricians spun sticks and brushes in front of the lights to simulate the headlights of oncoming traffic.

Brando did not like the scene as written and told Schulberg. The screenwriter was already annoyed because Brando had been ad-libbing a lot of his dialogue during the shoot. Kazan called a hasty meeting. "So what don't you like, Marlon?"

"Well, I don't think I could be saying, 'Awww, Charley, I coulda been a contender,' when a gun is being pressed against my ribs and the guy sticking me with the gun is my brother."

There was a long pause, and then Kazan suggested, "Why don't you improvise?"

What followed became one of the most unforgettable expressions of self-awareness on the part of a male hero in the history of American film, "the contrast of the tough-guy front and the extreme delicacy and gentle cast of his behavior," Kazan wrote in *A Life*. "What other actor, when his brother draws a pistol to force him to do something shameful, would put his hand on the gun and push it away with the gentleness of a caress? Who else could read, 'Oh, Charley,' in a tone of reproach that is so loving and so melancholy, and suggests that terrific depth of pain? I didn't direct that; Marlon showed me, as he often did, how the scene should be performed. I never could have told him how to do that scene as well as he did it."

As soon as Brando's close-up was done, "Marlon left to

keep his daily appointment with the shrink," Kazan says. Steiger didn't know why Brando walked off, so he took it as a personal affront. Kazan then stepped forward and read Brando's lines for Steiger's close-up, "which Rod did brilliantly." But Steiger was furious and never forgave either man.

Playing Terry Malloy in *On the Waterfront* was the peak of Brando's career, but after filming he'd sometimes wander the streets till dawn, or he'd go back to his apartment and hang on the telephone with someone till he dozed off. Occasionally he'd appear at a Mailer party and just sit there "like a buddha." Sometimes he'd play his congas for hours, hoping he'd find relief, beating out the rhythms he'd learned at Dunham's.

It kept getting harder and harder to act, to pull the emotional internal stuff out of him, although Kazan marveled at his surprising delicacy. When Brando filmed one of the most powerful scenes in the movie, in which he discovers his brother's dead body, left by union thugs to hang from a hook, at first he barely touches him. Then he puts his hands on the wall on either side of him but doesn't look at him. When he lifts him off the hook, he drapes his brother's hands around his neck; it's almost like an embrace. "It's a kind of symmetry that gives a mythic feeling to the entire picture," Jeff Young writes. But afterward Brando, exhausted by what the scene had taken out of him, visited the actress Barbara Baxley and kept repeating, "I don't think I'm good enough. I don't think I'm good enough."

*

He told another friend his daily sessions with Mittelmann were reducing him to a state of near panic. The most legendary of those anxiety attacks had occurred in the middle of one of his all-night walks when he ran to Stella Adler's apartment building and bellowed out her name—"Stella!"—from the street, as if he were playing Stanley. The rumor went around that he and Adler had been lovers and she'd finally rejected him and he was in such despair that he knelt outside her door crying out her name until she took him inside.

Brando has always denied that he and Adler had an affair, but he often visited Adler and Clurman, who were like a surrogate family to him. Clurman in fact wrote later of conversations they had had over the years, beginning about the time of *Truckline Cafe.* Back then Brando "sorrowfully confessed he'd smoked pot, and with similar overtones of guilt, admitted to sexual promiscuity." By the time of *Waterfront* he was starting to verbalize his huge ambivalence toward acting. He wanted to be taken seriously in whatever he did. But wasn't his *talent* huge enough for him to take it seriously? Why couldn't he take pride in that? Clurman wrote, "Yes, there is something in Marlon that *resents* acting, yet he cannot help but be an actor. He thinks acting 'sickly.' He'd rather 'do something for the world.'...There is nothing phony about this....However, his innermost core, secret even to himself, can find its outlet only through acting. And it is precisely because his acting has its source in suffering, the display of which he unwittingly resists, that it acquires its enormous power. Acting of this sort is instinct, with the stuff of humanity; it is not illustrative, it is creative."

*

Brando and Kazan worked very hard together in *On the Waterfront*. It was perhaps their most important collaboration, but their relationship was no longer intimate. On location the two men were extremely cordial to each other; once the director even persuaded Brando to join him for lunch with a bunch of gangsters. He had to get permission from the Mafia to shoot on the Hudson River docks. "Although Gadg had turned his friends in to the House committee over communism, he didn't even blink at having to cooperate with the Cosa Nostra," Brando writes. "By his own standards, it would seem that this was an act of remarkable hypocrisy, but when Gadg wanted to make a picture and had to move some furniture around to do so, he was perfectly willing."

Sometimes during filming Kazan would fling his arm around Brando's shoulder. Sometimes Brando would give him a lift in his limousine, and they would kid about their suspicion that the chauffeur driving them was a spy for Sam Spiegel (as he turned out to be).

Kazan said, "Marlon was perfect as Terry. Frank Sinatra would have been wonderful, but Marlon was more vulnerable. He had this great range of violent emotions to draw from. He had more schism, more pain, and so much shame— the actor who played Terry had to have a lot of shame. Where Marlon got it, I don't know."

Brando always praised Kazan as "the best director I have ever worked with," but he left it at that. However, throughout the film, he kept telling Kazan that the only reason he agreed to work with him again was so that he could continue his psychoanalysis in New York.

*

On the Waterfront completed filming at the end of December. It had been a cold and dangerous shoot. "The mob was always watching," Kazan said.

Bill Greaves, a black actor from the Actors Studio who often accompanied Brando when he went to Harlem to hear jazz, visited on location to observe the big fight scene that climaxes the picture. Invited to the makeshift dressing room in the Grand Hotel in Hoboken where Brando was being made up, Greaves watched "Marlon being daubed with fake blood. He is studying his face in the mirror and suddenly he tells the makeup man he's going to finish it up himself. He starts slathering guck on his face until fake blood is running down from his nose and the side of his mouth."

"'Hey, man,' I say, 'that is too much!'"

"He studies his face in the glass and shakes his head.

"We go out into the street and over to the piers. It is fuckin' freezing. Kazan comes over. I expect him to say, 'Marlon, wipe some of that stuff offa your face. It looks ridiculous.'

"But all Gadg says is 'Let's shoot it.'"

Then Greaves watched "one of the most savage beatings in movie history. It ends in a kind of pietà shot with Malden and Eva holding Marlon in their arms." He added that months later, when he saw *Waterfront* in a theater, "Marlon's face wasn't too bloody. The makeup was just perfect."

Soon after shooting was finished, Kazan was forced to assemble a quick rough cut of the film, because Spiegel wanted the composer Leonard Bernstein to score the picture. He thought it would help "sell" the movie. "So Lenny came," the director recalls. "I invited Marlon and Karl." Everyone sat silently in the tiny screening room. Every so often Spiegel would apologize to Bernstein because the cut was so clumsy and disjointed until Kazan shouted, "Shut up! Sam, this movie is damn *good*!"

When it went to black, Brando abruptly left, without so much as a good-bye to anyone. Malden ran after him. "What did you think?" he asked breathlessly. "I think it's terrific."

"Oh, it's in and out," Brando muttered, meaning he felt he was in and out of character, and then he disappeared. Later he wrote in his autobiography that he had hated his performance.

"Marlon often turns against some element of what he's been working on: a script, a director, or someone in the cast," Kazan said. "It seems to comfort him, this kind of acting out of a dissatisfaction. It's really a dissatisfaction about himself."

The following year *On the Waterfront*, made for only $850,000, opened and was a huge critical and commercial success. It was nominated for twelve Academy Awards. Brando, Kazan, Schulberg, and Saint all won Oscars. The picture has gone on to be listed as one of the most significant movies of the 1950s, and Marlon Brando's performance affected the way actors acted from then on. A review in the *Scotsman*, a newspaper in Edinburgh, summed it up: "This is the best sort of screen acting, always working inward, not building up, but chiseling away from the rock until we see the author's creation full size, and with all that is irrelevant cast aside."

10

AFTER SIX YEARS OF NONSTOP movie work, Brando's career was skyrocketing, but he was exhausted. Right after *Waterfront* finished, he dropped by the Actors Studio to relax with some of his old friends. The session was just breaking up as he arrived, and actors were milling around drinking coffee. Among them was Lou Gilbert, whom he'd worked with in *Streetcar* and Zapata. Gilbert saw him and made a comment about Kazan's being a stool pigeon, and Brando found himself crying out, "I'll kill you!" and then he ran out into the street with Gilbert stumbling after him, calling, "I'm sorry, Marlon....I'm sorry." Brando couldn't get over how embittered people were about Kazan, how disappointed.

He was feeling betrayed as well, on many levels. He'd just discovered that his father had totally mismanaged the funds in his Nebraska cattle ranch venture, so he needed $150,000 to salvage the deal. That was what Twentieth Century–Fox would pay Brando to star in *The Egyptian*.

It was the first such compromise he'd ever made, "doing crap for money." His misgivings grew after he flew out to

California in early January 1954 for costume fittings and rehearsals, and met his costar, Bella Darvi (Zanuck's latest mistress). Then he read *The Egyptian* script. "It is shit!" he cried out in dismay. After an unsatisfying conference with its director, Michael Curtiz, he boarded a train back to New York and convinced Dr. Mittelmann to write the following note: "Marlon Brando is sick and mentally confused and must remain in New York for treatment with me."

Fox responded by suing him for two million dollars, claiming that was what the studio would lose in preproduction costs if Brando didn't live up to his contract. His agents at MCA were apoplectic. Didn't he realize he was jeopardizing his entire career by taking such a foolhardy action? The newspapers got hold of the story and blew it out of all proportion, and a great deal of bad publicity ensued. Meanwhile Brando saw no one except Wally Cox and Phil Rhodes, and he hid out in various friends' apartments, including Barbara Baxley's Murray Hill studio, saying he was terrified Hollywood would destroy him.

He held his ground even after being served a summons. Occasionally he appeared at Stella Adler's for dinner. She introduced him to a petite nineteen-year-old artists' model, a French girl named Josanne Mariani-Berenger. They started seeing each other and were briefly engaged. But he could not commit himself to one woman and also spent time with Rita Moreno and Ellen Adler, as well as Movita.

Then, early in the spring of 1954, Dodie collapsed on a visit to her sister, Betty, in Pasadena. She was rushed to Huntington Memorial Hospital. Brando had last seen her when she and Senior had dropped by the set of *Waterfront*. Pale and drawn and chain-smoking, she would not admit she was suffering from hypertension, one of the effects of her long-term alcoholism.

Brando flew to California immediately, and he and his sisters took turns by Dodie's bedside. She slipped in and out of a coma for three weeks but managed to tell him to settle his differences with Fox, and she made him promise "to try and get along with people. Don't fight with them, Bud, try to get along with them."

On March 31, 1954, around 5:00 A.M., with her hand in his, Dodie murmured to her children, "I'm not scared, and you don't have to be," and breathed her last. Brando broke down and sobbed. After a few moments he managed to recover. He snipped a lock of her hair, took the pillow from under her head, and removed a beautiful aquamarine ring from her finger. He wandered out of the hospital into the dawn, thinking how gallant she had been. It seemed to him that everything in nature had become imbued with her spirit: the birds, the leaves on the trees, especially the wind. He remembered how she had taught him to love nature and animals and the closeness of the earth. All this helped him deal with his great loss.

Later he told Stella Adler that Dodie had taught him how to die. "Marlon didn't fall to pieces right away," Adler told Richard Schickel. "He was strong and controlled." But she predicted that the death of "this heavenly, girlish, lost creature would irrevocably change him. She was the symbol of many important things to Marlon—her passion for purity, her attitude towards animals and the earth and music."

Adler proved correct. "Marlon grew restless and unfocused

after his mother died," Sondra Lee recalled. "And he became more cynical."

The day after Dodie's death, he followed her wishes in seeking a settlement with Twentieth Century–Fox. Almost simultaneously, Fox announced it had ended its dispute with Marlon Brando: The two-million-dollar suit would be dropped, and he would star not in *The Egyptian* but in *Désirée*, a lavish, simpleminded CinemaScope spectacle based on a best-selling historical novel. Brando would play Napoleon, opposite Jean Simmons as Désirée. She moons over Napoleon throughout the entire movie.

Brando worried about playing "the cliché idea of this emperor, hand-inside-of-jacket kind of stuff." He spent a lot of time fussing with false noses and makeup and much padding around his waist, and he developed a Claude Rains English accent. He had endless disagreements with the director of *Désirée*, Henry Koster, who considered himself an expert on Napoleon. The two men argued about who knew more.

Koster, a mild-mannered man who had directed Deanna Durbin musicals, became the first but not the last director to be tested, and to some degree victimized, by Brando. "Marlon was always having these power struggles with father figures," his friend the actor Sidney Armus recalled.

Armus was in Hollywood with Sondra Lee at the time, and they visited the set of *Désirée*. "This was a real turning point for Marlon," Armus recalled. "He was not concentrating. I think he decided to sell out. He played with water pistols on the set, and he sulked and wouldn't learn his lines. When I was there, I watched him toss a football between takes. 'I let the makeup play the part,' he told me, but he did seem to have a good time acting with Jean Simmons. He really liked her, and she liked him."

When *Désirée* opened, the critic Pauline Kael said, "The two stars [Brando and Simmons] play with conspiratorial charm, as if they'd been trapped in a joke and are trying to have as good a time as possible." The funniest bit came when he hands over his sword to Désirée and tells her in a crisp English accent, "Please don't treat it like an umbrella."

Other critics called *Désirée* "abysmal," but it grossed more than *On the Waterfront*.

Next Brando starred in Sam Goldwyn's production of the jaunty Frank Loesser musical *Guys and Dolls*, based on Damon Runyon's stories about lovable Broadway lowlifes. Frank Sinatra costarred as Nathan Detroit, who ran the "oldest established permanent floating crap game" in New York, with Jean Simmons as Sister Sarah, the sweet Salvation Army worker. Joseph L. Mankiewicz directed.

Brando played the wisecracking gambler Sky Masterson. "The only reason I played Sky," he told Truman Capote, "was to work in a lighter color—yellow. Before that, the brightest color I'd played in was red." In order to learn how to sing, he trained religiously with MGM's voice coach and endured dozens of takes, flubbing the lyrics constantly. He was very nervous, and he kept pleading that "they should get some-body else to sing."

Oddly enough, he felt more secure during the dance rou-tines, which he worked on with the choreographer Michael

Kidd, who told Peter Manso that "Marlon approached the numbers in acting terms."

While struggling to perfect the song-and-dance routine in "Luck Be a Lady," Brando sensed that the staging didn't "feel right." Kidd told Manso, "He was absolutely right." Kidd added that he'd been looking at it technically. "In New York I'd put Sky front-center so the audience could hear, which meant I was automatically repeating myself. Marlon came to me and said, 'Look, I wouldn't be doing it with all these people standing around. As Sky, I'd be thinking about my bet in private. I wouldn't expose myself.'"

Brando did not get along with Frank Sinatra, who was still furious that he'd lost the part of Terry Malloy in *Waterfront*. "When Marlon tried to make nice to Frank and asked him to run lines," Phil Rhodes recalls, "Frank says, 'Don't pull that Actors Studio shit on me.'"

By the end of filming Brando was complaining to Mankiewicz that he thought Sinatra's characterization of Nathan Detroit was wrong. "He's supposed to sing with a Bronx accent....But he's singing like a romantic lead. We can't have *two* romantic leads." Brando urged Mankiewicz to speak to Sinatra about this. "You speak to him, Marlon," Mankiewicz said.

Luckily, the two great stars had few scenes together, but Sinatra remained in an ugly mood throughout the shoot and refused to do any publicity. "Frank's the kind of person when he gets to heaven he's gonna be mad at God for making him bald," Brando joked.

By then he'd won the Oscar for *Waterfront,* and he'd been on CBS-TV's *Person to Person* with Ed Murrow, appearing with Senior and pointing to a portrait of his mother, saying he wished she could have been there to share in his triumph. He was briefly basking in his huge success. He even attended a big outdoor barbecue at the Goldwyns' and helped Mrs. Goldwyn charbroil steaks on the grill; she confided to him that she had never done a barbecue before.

Goldwyn was so pleased with *Guys and Dolls* that he gave Brando a Thunderbird car, which in return obligated him to do an enormous amount of publicity, including appearances in Las Vegas and on an ABC-TV special and attending the glittering premiere of the movie. "Marlon hated doing all this publicity. It unnerved him," Joe Mankiewicz said.

At the premiere of *Guys and Dolls* at the Capital Theater in New York on November 4, 1955, a crowd of thousands jammed both sides of Broadway, watching Brando's limousine inch forward down the street through a driving rain. Suddenly dozens of screaming fans broke through the barricades, clambered onto the hood of the car, and attempted to smash the windows. Brando commented afterward, "It was frightening, like being trapped inside a submarine."

When he finally emerged from his car, a great human roar reverberated throughout Times Square. Two mounted police galloped between the mob and Brando, while fifty more policemen managed to push him inside the theater's lobby. At the opening-night party he managed to joke, "This is the last publicity I do for that Thunderbird."

Guys and Dolls was a big commercial hit. It received four Oscar nominations. Richard Schickel later said, "Brando is marvelous in what is probably his most underrated performance this side of *Mutiny on the Bounty*." Bosley Crowther wrote in the *New York Times*, "Brando brings a kind of sweet, heavy, comic seriousness to the role of gambler Sky Masterson. His singing is endearingly his own, high pitched, soft and sincere." However, when Brando heard it, he joked, "My voice sounds like the wail of a bagpipe through wet tissues."

He was now receiving six thousand fan letters a week, and the *Independent Film Journal* named him its top money-making star in 1955, more popular than James Stewart, John Wayne, or Gary Cooper.

But 1955 was one of the worst years in the motion-picture business. Hollywood was being reconstituted. The studios, by government decree, had divested themselves of their lucrative theater chains, and television was challenging the film industry and taking away its audience. Millions of families now sat in their living rooms, hypnotized in front of flickering sets watching *I Love Lucy*. Movies were no longer the great American pastime. Hollywood fought back with CinemaScope and epics like *The Robe*.

Shortly after he won the Academy Award, Brando formed his own production company, Pennebaker Inc., with a friend, George Englund. It was supposedly a means of supporting Senior, as well as a tax shelter, but Brando also wanted to develop projects for himself and to make movies "that had social value and would improve the world." Richard Schickel has commented that from here on, "almost all Brando's career problems stemmed from his insistence that his movies make some useful, uplifting statement. This vitiated both his powers of choice and his powers as a performer." Be that as it may, MCA structured the deal, and Paramount supported

Pennebaker for an unspoken number of pictures. Marlon Brando was a big star, and the studio wanted to keep him happy.

For a long time he naively hoped he would continue to find decent scripts to work with and directors who would allow him to stretch his remarkable talent. But after 1955 the independent, tough-minded movies he was best suited for— small black-and-white films *about* something, like *Waterfront*—were hard to come by. The exceptions, like *Sweet Smell of Success,* were few and far between.

He soon traveled more than twenty thousand miles, visiting such Third World countries as Indonesia, Borneo, and Pakistan with the scriptwriter Stewart Stern, hoping to film a documentary about U.S. intervention in Southeast Asia. He also maintained he wanted to do a movie about Native Americans, as well as another movie about the kidnapping of UN workers in Third World countries. None of these movies was ever made, but Pennebaker did produce two features, *Shake Hands with the Devil,* with Don Murray as an activist priest, and *Paris Blues,* about jazz musicians. It had originally been developed for Brando and Marilyn Monroe, but they lost interest, and Paul Newman starred in it.

Even though his father had lost a fortune in the Nebraska cattle ranch venture, as well as in a bogus gold mine scheme, Brando put Senior in as president of Pennebaker, in charge of handling the administrative end of the business. He hoped that giving him that job might lessen the strain between them. Instead their relationship grew more edgy. Senior was critical of the idealistic projects Brando dreamed of doing in film; he thought his son's money could be spent more wisely.

They shared offices in the same suite on the Paramount studio lot, and occasionally they received each other's mail by mistake. When this was discovered, Brando stormed into his father's office and ordered, "I want you to change your name."

Senior raised an eyebrow. "You know, Bud, I've had the name for about twenty-five years longer than you have," he declared. "I suggest *you* change your name." He often confided wearily, "The worst mistake I ever made was giving my son my name."

The two men continued to have problems. They had an ugly row at a party Brando gave for some of his friends at his father's new apartment in West Hollywood. The guests became so noisy Senior asked them to leave. Charles Higham reports in his Brando biography, "When Marlon wouldn't tell his friends to go home, Senior slapped him violently across the face and almost knocked him over. Marlon turned pale with anger, but didn't strike back."

Every time he laid eyes on his father, Brando was reminded that Dodie was gone. He remained haunted by the memory of her songs, of her gardens, and of the terrible struggles and disappointments she had had in her marriage. He kept her aquamarine ring close by; it had started changing color from greeny blue to cloudy gray.

While he was in mourning, he spent time with the playwright Clifford Odets. This once-dynamic wild-haired man, who had written *Golden Boy* and Awake and Sing and had been the Group Theatre's greatest hope, was now living in Hollywood, grinding out rewrites of screenplays for Elvis

Presley and selling paintings from his collection to make ends meet.

The two sat for hours talking. Odets was obsessed with the idea of how an artist maintains his potency. His idol was Beethoven. He believed that the composer had sacrificed everything for his music: "Every atom of his sensitivity and brain tissues was shot through with his music. He *cohabitated* with his music...." He rambled on and on about how one should listen to Beethoven. "You will understand his music after you reach forty. You will be startled and entranced, because the beauty and the grandeur of the music are an expression of such a life force, it will be hard to bear." Odets wanted to write a screenplay of Beethoven's life for Brando. "Only a great artist can portray another great artist," he said. But he never completed the script.

One evening after dinner Brando drove Odets home and suddenly began reminiscing about his mother, about her talent and her despair. "I loved her more than anything," he declared. "I thought I could help her solve her problems." He relived the times as a young boy when he'd actually had to carry her home from bars near Chicago. Then suddenly after she joined AA she seemed not to need him. "I thought that meant she no longer loved me...."

As he spoke, he began to sob. His vision was blinded by tears and the car careered from side to side, racing up and down Hollywood's steep dark hills. Odets was terrified they might be killed, but suddenly Brando regained his composure. His sobbing ceased, and they drove on into the night.

11

BRANDO FIRST SAW TWENTY-TWO-YEAR-OLD Anna
Kashfi in the Paramount commissary, in November 1955.
Dressed in a red silk sari, she was frail and olive-skinned, with
huge dark eyes and a beguiling manner. He decided she was
the most beautiful woman in the world.

At the time she was making a movie with Spencer Tracy
titled *The Mountain*. From a press agent Brando learned
that she'd been born in Calcutta and educated in a French
convent there. She supposedly spoke eight languages. She'd
been discovered by a talent scout while she was giving a
dance recital in London. Brando assumed she was from a
fine Hindu family.

He began taking her out for lobster dinners with his Pennebaker partner, George Englund, and for sedate drives around
Beverly Hills in his Thunderbird. His other car was a beat-up
Volkswagen littered with old newspapers, hamburger wrap-
pings, and empty beer cans. The white Thunderbird he used
for special occasions, he told her.

Not long after they began seeing each other, he had to leave to film *The Teahouse of the August Moon* in Japan. The movie was based on a hit Broadway play by John Patrick, and Brando starred as Sakini, a wily Asian interpreter for the U.S. Army, which occupied postwar Okinawa. When the production was rained out in Japan, he returned to complete the movie at MGM.

By then Kashfi had been hospitalized with tuberculosis. The recuperation took five months. Brando visited her every night, straight from the set of *Teahouse*. He'd often come in costume and full makeup, "a rubber lid around his eyes, protruding teeth, a wig, and layers of yellowish greasepaint." He spoke in a mad accent that was more a parlor trick than a true performance (he'd asked a Japanese friend to speak his lines into a tape recorder, and then he mimicked them). He loved repeating the aphorism in the movie "Pain makes man think, thought makes man wise, and wisdom makes life endurable." Once in Kashfi's hospital room, Brando would scuttle around with great bunches of fresh flowers, candy, books. He even brought a 16-millimeter camera so he could screen some of his favorite movies for her, such as *Singing in the Rain*.

Soon he was blurting out how much he cared for her and that he wanted to marry her. He gave her his mother's pillow and her ring. He said, "I wish Dodie was alive to meet you. She would have loved you. You and she are so alike." Then he cried, "I'm glad she's dead! If she was alive, I never could have loved you. She wouldn't have let me go."

When Kashfi left the hospital, Brando arranged to have her spend the night at his aunt Betty's in Eagle Rock. "She lent me a nightgown," Kashfi writes in her autobiography, "and I fell asleep and had a vivid dream about Dodie coming to see me. When I woke up, I told Betty my dream, and I described Dodie—blonde, tall, sort of beat up but attractive, and Aunt Betty said, 'Oh, yeah, that's her.' And she mentioned she'd lent me *Dodie*'s nightgown. It was my first extra-sensory experience, and I found it unsettling."

Brando rented an apartment for her in the same West Hollywood complex his father was living in, a 1930s-style place built around a courtyard and a swimming pool. Kashfi met Senior, whom she described as a brooding old man with the "residue of debauchery etched across his face."

Every so often she would hear Senior arguing with Alice Marchak, an attractive former MCA secretary Brando had introduced to his father. Once she heard Marchak screaming that she wanted to kill herself. Apparently Marchak was jealous because Senior had become interested in another woman, and she was threatening to "slit her wrists" in his apartment. Brando subsequently hired her as his personal secretary, and she remained with him for the next twenty-five years.

As soon as he finished *Teahouse,* Brando went directly into *Sayonara.* Set in the closing days of the Korean War, the film was about bigotry in the U.S. Army. Brando played Gruver, a jet pilot from Texas who falls in love with a Japanese dancer. He'd initially refused the role until the screenwriter changed the ending so that Gruver would marry the Japanese dancer.

In January 1957 Brando had to go to Japan to make the film, and for company he took his father and his aunt along because he wanted to "educate them with travel." His entourage included his friend Carlo Fiore, who'd sworn off drugs and had been hired as dialogue coach, and Brando's ex-girl-friend Celia Webb, who was serving as a secretary.

He wrote Kashfi long, impassioned letters, telling her that he was becoming increasingly dissatisfied with the script and was doing extensive rewrites himself. He fought constantly with the director, Josh Logan. In the end Brando's performance is remarkable for its blend of amiability and discomfort.

Midway through filming, Truman Capote showed up, asking to interview him. Logan pleaded with Brando not to do the interview. "He'll destroy you," he warned. Brando just laughed, and the following evening he and Capote talked and drank vodka for almost five hours.

The Brando profile, entitled "The Duke in His Domain," is considered a journalistic tour de force. In it, Capote describes an overweight, self-indulgent movie star, sitting amid a messy hotel suite, ordering too much food ("'soup, beefsteak with french fries, three orders of vegetables, a plate of spaghetti, rolls and butter, and apple pie with ice cream,' honey"). He says he is trying to write a screenplay called *Burst of Vermillion,* which he insists will deal with racial prejudice in a different way.

Brando confides that the last eight years of his life have been a mess. He speaks of his analysis: "I was afraid of it at first. Afraid it might destroy the impulses that made me creative, an artist. A sensitive person receives fifty impressions where someone else only may get seven. Sensitive people are so vulnerable; they're so easily brutalized and hurt because they *are* sensitive. The more sensitive you are, the more certain you are to be brutalized, develop scabs. Never evolve.

Never allow yourself to feel anything, because you always feel too much. Analysis helps. It helped me. But, still, the last eight, nine years I've been pretty mixed up, a mess pretty much...."

After talking for nearly five hours, he ends by saying he is unable to love or trust anyone.

When the piece was published, in November 1957, it created a sensation in the media, and Brando's public image was irrevocably changed. "A real vivisection," the gossip columnist Dorothy Kilgallen crowed.

Brando was enraged when he read it. "That little bastard spent half the night telling me his problems. I felt the least I could do was tell him a few of mine. I'll kill him!" he shouted to Josh Logan, who answered, "You should have done that before you let him come into your room."

He considered suing Capote, but in the end he dismissed the idea, and when someone asked him, "What are you going to do?" he shrugged. "I think I'm going to beat him with a wet noodle." Meanwhile *Sayonara* was a huge hit at the box office, and Brando was nominated for the fifth time for an Academy Award.

He was working nonstop. In June 1957 he flew to Paris to film *The Young Lions,* a movie based on Irwin Shaw's best-selling novel, "which attempted to encompass the entire experience of World War II into a single volume." Edward Dmytryk directed.

The story followed the lives of three young men: Michael, a nightclub entertainer, played by Dean Martin; Noah Ackerman, a shy Jewish GI, played by Montgomery Clift; and, as

Shaw originally intended, a passionate Nazi officer named Christian Diestl, played by Marlon Brando. As soon as he read the script, Brando told Carlo Fiore that he was going to "turn this Nazi heel into a tragic hero" who believed Hitler was a positive force because he had given the Germans a sense of purpose.

Once Brando had seen a beautiful blond boy in an old German movie and had fallen in love with his face, which he decided to replicate for Christian; he would dye his hair platinum and have Phil Rhodes give him a noble "John Barrymore nose." He demanded rewrites to fit his vision of the character. Dmytryk later admitted to Montgomery Clift that he had agreed to them so that Brando would star in the film.

In a debate on CBS-TV, Irwin Shaw accused Brando of changing the role because he wanted to appear sympathetic on-screen. Brando retorted that he hadn't wanted to play Christian Diestl as a nasty, vicious cliché of evil and that Shaw knew nothing about the character. "It's my character," Shaw replied angrily. "I created him."

"Nobody creates a character but an actor," Brando argued. "I play the role; now he exists. He's my creation."

But his romanticized interpretation continued to infuriate Shaw and also Montgomery Clift, who thought that idealizing Diestl would undercut the story. The two actors argued, but Brando wouldn't listen; he was planning a very dramatic death at the end of the picture, by rolling down a hill with his arms outstretched like a Christ figure. "If he does that, I walk off the movie," Clift threatened. (Ultimately Brando's Diestl was shot in the head by Dean Martin.)

While Brando's performance does capture the confusion of

a man torn between his dedicated patriotism and his essential decency, nobody—especially friends like Maureen Stapleton, who found it offensive and with whom, months later, he had a screaming argument—would ever buy his concept of "Nazi-as-saint." He finally admitted to her that he'd forced Dmytryk to agree to his changes, and then he cried out, "If it had been Gadg, he wouldn't have let me do it."

He was then at the height of his fame. Celebrity was a nightmare for him. It was an embarrassment; it was dangerous. While he was filming in Paris, he was mobbed, and fans tore off his coat and ripped his shirt. He grew increasingly paranoid, believing that most people he knew were using him for money or fame or status. He was starting to understand manipulation and hypocrisy from the inside. "His eyes changed," Pat Cox said. "No more shyness, no more vulnerability. He looked at everybody with a lot of confidence. But also pity too. Like he felt sorry for you."

He describes himself at that time as being "a bomb waiting to go off." He had a terrible temper, and it was usually directed at men, and a lot of the time at paparazzi. Once, in Hollywood, he knocked a photographer's camera out of his hand, and later, in Rome, he actually choked a photographer who was trying to take a picture of him and one of his many women.

To protect himself from the public during the filming of *The Young Lions,* he surrounded himself with close friends like Christian Marquand and makeup man Phil Rhodes and his wife, Marie. Rhodes had said he would not travel without

Marie, so Brando arranged for her to be his stand-in, a job she held for many years.

Soon after he completed *The Young Lions,* Brando married for the first time. His wife was Anna Kashfi, who'd discovered she was pregnant. He had doubts whether he should be married. He talked about it a lot to his sisters: Could he really trust Anna? Live with her forever? He decided he would give the marriage a year at least. He wanted to do the right thing for the baby.

The ceremony was supposed to take place early on October 11, 1957, at the modest home of Brando's aunt, Betty Lindemeyer. Guests included his sister Jocelyn and her new husband, writer Eliot Asinof. Senior was not invited; "I'll bury him first," Brando said. Kashfi's only guests were the western novelist Louis L'Amour and his wife, Kathy.

Everything was delayed when the flowers Kashfi wanted for her bouquet, a rare strain of lily of the valley, could be ordered only from a florist in San Francisco. So, according to Kashfi, "We sat around drinking champagne until the lilies arrived, 48 hours later. By then everyone was understandably quite drunk."

There was no honeymoon. The couple had forgotten to make any plans. So they drove aimlessly all over Los Angeles, Brando still wearing his wedding attire of dark suit, black cape, and homburg. Finally they spent the night at Jay Kanter's home in Beverly Hills, and that weekend they drove down to Palm Springs and stayed with the L'Amours.

When they returned to Hollywood, Brando escaped to his sister Jocelyn's. He crawled through the window of her house, dropped to the floor, and collapsed onto the sofa. "Well, I did it." He grinned. "I got married. Now what do I do?"

By the following week the newspapers had got wind of the nuptials, and a William O'Callaghan living in Wales announced to a London tabloid that he was Anna's father, and her name was really Joanne O'Callaghan, and, as far as he knew, she had no Indian blood. She had been raised in Calcutta, yes, because he'd had a job there as an engineer. Her mother, Selma Gouse, was English.

Kashfi angrily stuck to her story that she was a Darjeeling-born Buddhist of pure Indian parentage. William O'Callaghan was her stepfather. Her real father, an architect, David Kashfi, had died early in 1955; Marlon had known all about it, she said. The name Joanne O'Callaghan was on her passport to circumvent the quota of Indians admitted to the United States. Marlon knew about that too, she said.

Brando tried to be supportive, but secretly he hired detectives to find out the truth. Nothing ever came of the investigations, and Kashfi remained defensive about her past. Senior thought she was "nothing but a gold digger." Still, for a while she and Brando were wined and dined all over Hollywood because everyone wanted to meet the exotic Indian woman Marlon Brando had married. Some evenings they drove over to Humphrey Bogart's elegant mansion in Holmby Hills. Then, while Kashfi gossiped with Lauren Bacall, Brando and Bogart played "sadistic" games of chess for hours.

Chess was a lifelong passion with Brando, who played between takes on every movie set and even for hours at home by himself. He later told writer Larry Grobel, "Nobody knows what makes a good chess player. Architects make good chess players. It doesn't have to do with intelligence, it has to do with a sense of space."

On May 16, 1958, Christian Devi Brando was born in Cedars of Lebanon Hospital. Brando had tears in his eyes when he held his tiny son in his arms. "The baby is beautiful," he told Anna. "Thank God he looks more like you than me." The couple had secreted themselves in a separate room from Anna's actual room because photographers disguised as doctors were roaming the maternity ward, trying to locate the infant.

For the next couple of months Brando and Kashfi lived together in a rented Japanese-style house with white silk walls, originally built by Howard Hughes at the top of Mulholland Drive. The place had a breathtaking view of all of Los Angeles, but they were fighting so much they didn't enjoy it. Kashfi disliked the constant flow of people in and out. Dean Martin came over for acting lessons, and for a while Maureen Stapleton lived in the spare bedroom, until Kashfi pointedly asked her to leave. Brando had hired too many servants: two gardeners, a cook, and several maids. None of them had enough to do, so they were starting to quarrel. Ultimately Kashfi fired most of them. Brando didn't seem to notice. He was a cordial, undemanding boss, but he often disappeared. He had started spending half his nights out with France Nuyen, the beautiful young Asian star.

In June 1958 another drama erupted. "Marlon thrived on dramas," Kashfi said. Senior married thirty-eight-year-old "Anichka," Anna Frenke Paramore, the daughter of Gene Frenke, a wealthy real estate investor. He phoned from New

York to tell Brando the news. Kashfi recounted in her memoir that Brando said, "Hi, Pop. I hope you'll be happy," and then slammed down the phone and yelled, "Why did you make me talk to him? That God damn son of a bitch, I can't stand him. And the way he treated my mother...to hell with him!"

Nevertheless, Brando and Senior and their wives began socializing, often joined by Wally and Pat Cox, since they lived in houses not far from one another in Coldwater Canyon. However, there was still unrelieved tension between father and son. "They would be in the same room together, and you could literally *feel* the hostility," Pat Cox said. "It was really unnerving. But they remained fascinated with each other and couldn't get enough of each other, even though there was no love lost."

Their hostility carried over into the Pennebaker office, with Senior disapproving of "Marlon's nonstop screwing and his lack of interest in the business." Brando, for his part, had decided that his father was so ineffectual in supervising his financial affairs, as well as in managing Pennebaker, that he wanted him fired; his partners, Walter Seltzer and George Glass, persuaded him "to hold off." The irony was that Brando himself was ineffectual, too, and refused to make any decisions regarding production.

For several years Paramount had bankrolled Pennebaker, which had yet to be profitable. In order for the company to justify its existence and maximize tax benefits, Brando had to put himself in a Pennebaker film. He finally did this at the eleventh hour, choosing to star in *One-Eyed Jacks,* a classic western melodrama of betrayal and revenge, reminiscent of the legend of Pat Garrett and Billy the Kid. Brando hired

Niven Busch to write the first draft of the screenplay, and Sam Peckinpah came in to write a second. Stanley Kubrick agreed to direct, mainly because he wanted to work with Brando. "Everybody still wanted to work with Brando," Pat Cox said.

Matters were temporarily smoothed over at Pennebaker, but then Senior fired a friend of Brando's who was working at the company. Senior was "sick and tired of the people Bud associated with. They are nothing but trash." Brando immediately reinstated his friend. Then he marched into his father's office and told him off, saying in effect how he'd ruined Dodie's life, turned his daughters into alcoholics, and taken every opportunity to make Brando feel inadequate. "I told him...he was cold, unloving, selfish, infantile, terminally despicable and self-absorbed," he writes in his autobiography. "In three hours I did what in thirty-three years I had never been able to, yet the whole time I was scared. I was frightened of what *he* would do to *me*. I had always been overwhelmed and intimidated by him, but the more I talked, the more strength and conviction I gained."

However, in the days that followed, Brando experienced "aftershocks from what I had done. I thought the sky was going to fall on me because of what I had said." He adds that after that he kept his father "on a tight leash so that he could never come near me and never get too far away. I had him under control and never let him go."

12

MEANWHILE BRANDO REMAINED IN the Mulholland Drive house, which he bought and ultimately turned into a fortress, and he continued working on various versions of the *One-Eyed Jacks* screenplay with Stanley Kubrick. But nothing seemed to be coming together. They disagreed on casting and on the story line. After six months, Kubrick threw up his hands. "I still can't figure out what this movie is about."

"It's about the $350,000 I've spent so far," Brando said chuckling. He was referring to his estimate of development costs.

That was when Kubrick left and signed immediately to direct *Spartacus*. He told friends later that he sensed that "Marlon wanted to direct the movie all along anyway."

Brando *had* wanted to direct. He was thrilled to be directing, to have total control, and he became involved with every aspect of the movie, from costumes to sets to lighting. He even had a dozen horses brought up to Mulholland Drive, and they trotted around the garden while he "auditioned" them. And he had lots of meetings with his crew; he would call meetings to order in the dining room by striking a big brass gong.

He decided on the stunning locations in Death Valley, where he often went motorcycling, and on the Monterey coast. The spectacular scenery would be ravishingly photographed by Charles Lang. Before filming, Brando went home to the farm in Mundelein and practiced using a movie camera so he could figure out the compositional dynamics of space.

Mostly he labored over more drafts of the screenplay with Calder Willingham, whom he eventually dismissed, and finally with Guy Trosper. It was a very personal screenplay. At its best, it is an extraordinary meditation on two of Brando's favorite subjects, the ambiguity of human nature and the terrible costs of loyalty and revenge. The movie is littered with autobiographical references that seem inspired by Brando's love-hate relationship with Senior. In the movie, Brando was to star as Rio, outlaw and womanizer, and Karl Malden was to play the unctuous villain, Dad, his partner in robbing Mexican banks, who then betrays him and administers the most brutal of Brando's on-screen beatings. In the end Rio kills him and goes off with Dad's daughter.

What's so sinister and fascinating about the subtext of the screenplay is Rio's (Brando's?) implacable certainty that a man can stay angry forever and enjoy it.

Shooting began on *One-Eyed Jacks* on December 2, 1958, and continued for six months, a very long time even in those days. The studio became increasingly concerned by Brando's need to wait for hours for the right light or for the perfect cloud formations above the ocean. He dislocated his shoulder showing Malden how to snap a bullwhip. One day an executive came by and watched Brando direct for a while. "You're looking into the wrong end of the viewfinder," he said.

"Holy shit!" Brando joked. "Maybe that's why the picture is so late."

Even so, Malden maintained, "I thought Marlon was a terrific director. I trusted his eyes. He told me right off, 'I want the makeup man to work on you. I see you with a bushy mane like a lion.'" Soon fitted with a hairpiece, Malden pronounced Brando's choice "brilliant. He knew exactly how to frame a shot pictorially. He was always surprising us." Malden continued, "And he improvised with everybody, even the extras. He used to say to the cast, 'Forget the script; that's what they did in silent movies. Do what you want for starters. You can be freer if you improvise. There are less restrictions.'"

The budget had been two million; it soared to six million. Eventually Paramount, which was distributing the picture, pressured Brando to cut two crucial scenes in the movie, "which took the guts out of the story," Malden remembers. The cast protested by going on strike, but that made no difference, and Paramount cut the two scenes. Brando, reacting to the pressure, started overeating. Karl Malden recalls seeing him at a five-star restaurant in Monterey, gorging on two enormous meals, one after the other, which he topped off with apple pie à la mode washed down with an entire quart of milk.

Halfway through the production of *One-Eyed Jacks*, Anna Kashfi walked out on the marriage. She could no longer tolerate Brando's philandering. They subsequently divorced, and she was given sole custody of Christian and awarded $440,000 in support over the next ten years, including $1,000 a month for child support. From then on there were frequent custody battles over their son, attempted break-ins, and even attempted kidnappings, with Brando demanding his allotted time with Christian, which he often missed when he was away filming. Once Kashfi tried to hit Brando over the head when they were leaving her lawyers' office after an especially ugly confrontation. Photographers snapped a candid of the couple that landed on the front pages of tabloids around the world.

But it was little Christian who suffered the most, being shuttled back and forth from the Mulholland Drive house to Kashfi's various rented homes, where he was cared for by an assortment of nannies and maids. He soon became "disoriented, confused, and impossible to handle," Pat Cox said.

By the time he completed *One-Eyed Jacks,* Brando had shot more than a million feet of film. The rough assemblage took five hours to watch. The late photographer Sam Shaw, one of the few people to see this version, called it "a masterpiece, a real romantic western." But various Paramount executives claimed it was just a mess of film.

Brando attempted to cut it himself to a reasonable length, but he was inexperienced in editing. Besides, he'd started commuting to Wilton, Connecticut, to film Tennessee Williams's *The Fugitive Kind,* with Anna Magnani. Brando was receiving one million dollars for playing Val Xavier, a guitar-picking singer who wears a snakeskin jacket and comes to a brutal end. Later he told people he'd sold his soul so he could pay his alimony.

For a while he continued to act in *The Fugitive Kind* and to edit *One-Eyed Jacks,* but he could not do both. Near collapse, he let Paramount take over the picture. He was bitterly disappointed in himself and in Hollywood. He had dreamed of directing a picture he could be proud of, but when the studio insisted on tacking on a "happy" ending a year after the movie was completed, Brando's disillusionment with the film industry increased.

Malden believes, "If we'd made it the way Marlon wanted it to be made, like a Greek tragedy, it could have been a breakthrough western. It could have been a classic."

Most critics were fierce in their denunciation when it was finally released in 1961—"a bad movie with a great many insights," said *The New Yorker*—but it probably contains the most accurate on-screen portrait of Brando at the time, a man with an unforgettable face about to spoil and grow fat, a man seemingly incapable or unwilling to project love or desire to anyone else on the screen; that strain became in Brando's work "a kind of sadism mixed with masochism."

On June 4, 1960, Brando married Movita in Mexico in a secret ceremony. He set her up in a comfortable house in Coldwater Canyon and gave her a generous allowance, but he never lived with her. Soon she announced she had borne him a son named Miko, and a few years later, a daughter, Rebecca.

He was always an indulgent, concerned, but often absent father. He behaved very differently around kids. He was at ease and playful, totally losing himself in their whimsical worlds. He saw himself as a real paterfamilias. Eventually he had nine children, not counting those he adopted, but a close friend says, "Nobody really knows how many kids Marlon has. He might not know either."

He also had several sets of surrogate parents for himself. Makeup man Phil Rhodes and his wife, Maria, were one set; Wally Cox and his wife, Pat, another. Brando alternated between the two couples, traveling with them, practically living with them.

"Marlon was at our house more than his own," Pat Cox recalled recently. "When we were away somewhere, he'd break in, and when we got back, we'd often find him lolling on our couch, eating peanut butter out of a jar."

Over the years Brando watched helplessly as Wally became an alcoholic. Hollywood didn't know how to use this true original, this eccentric talent, and it ended up exploiting Cox and turning him into a cliché of himself. After *Mr. Peepers,* his career floundered. He flopped in Las Vegas, and then he did guest shots on various TV shows, small parts in films, and the voice of the cartoon character Underdog. He had a comic triumph as the "persnickety bird watcher" P. Caspar Biddle on two episodes of *The Beverly Hillbillies.* He hadn't really wanted to be a performer, but he never knew exactly what he wanted to do. Like Brando, he was interested in a multitude of things. Brando always tried to get him work in his movies when he could. They were rarely out of touch.

For the last years of his life Wally was on the TV program *Hollywood Squares* five days a week, fifty-two weeks a year. He ad-libbed and joked, and audiences thought he was hilarious, even though he was half bombed most of the time. But it was good money, and he had plenty of time to do what he wanted to do, which was to "walk in the woods with Marlon," naming every wildflower in the earth, and to invent curious things. He had a rope suspended from the ceiling of his living room so he could swing from one end of the house to the other. Once he wired all his telephone lines to the trees in his garden, so that when the phones rang, they rang outside and reverberated quite magically in the leafy branches.

Another time he and Brando and Ursula Andress recorded the entire King James Version of the Bible, playing every devil and every saint. The recording has since been lost, much to Brando's dismay.

Wally and Pat frequently baby-sat for Miko, who, when he was a little boy, could be quite disruptive and unruly. He was undisciplined, and he enjoyed biting people. Cox, a mild-mannered man, took it for as long as he could, but one day when he was talking on the phone to Brando, he confided, "Marlon, I really dislike Miko."

"What did you say?" Brando intoned ominously.

Cox repeated, "I dislike Miko."

"I'm coming right over!" Brando told him, and slammed down the phone.

Cox looked at Pat. "I'm afraid our friendship is over," he said, "but I have to tell him what I feel."

Brando lived just up the hill from the Coxes, so he was inside their living room in a matter of minutes.

"Repeat what you said about Miko," he ordered.

Cox stood his ground. "I really dislike Miko," he said. "In fact I cannot stand the little bugger."

With that, Brando collapsed in a chair. "What a relief!" he groaned. "Because I don't much like him either. Now I don't feel so guilty." After Miko grew up, he and Brando became close; he is the one son Brando sees consistently.

Sam Spiegel wanted Brando for *Lawrence of Arabia,* but after a meeting in Paris with director David Lean, Brando decided he didn't want to be in the desert with camels for a year and signed to star in *Mutiny on the Bounty* instead. It was to be a remake of the MGM classic, which had starred Clark Gable and Charles Laughton. Brando agreed to play Fletcher Christian on one condition: that the screenplay explore *what happened after the mutiny.* What did the sailors do after they reached Pitcairn? What made them kill one another while living on an island paradise? (The trouble with this idea was that it destroyed the structural unity of the story, which climaxed with the noisy mutiny.)

The shoot began in October 1960 on the island of Tahiti, the Eden Brando had fantasized about as a teenager. The creamy sands, balmy weather, and the happiness of the natives with their "unmanaged faces" seemed like heaven on earth to him. He could walk barefoot into a bar or swim naked in the lagoon, and nobody even noticed him. Rejecting the stately home MGM had rented for him, he moved into a thatched hut on the beach, and every day after filming he'd put on a vivid sarong, play congas for hours, or go dancing. He soon fell in love with his female costar, nineteen-year-old half-Chinese, half-Polynesian Tarita Tumi Teriipaia, who had quit her job as a waitress to be in the movie.

Whenever he could, Brando explored the island. Not long

after he got there, he climbed to the highest mountain and saw in the distance an atoll stretching for some fifteen hundred acres. Named Tetiaroa, it was owned by Madame Duran, a blind woman who lived there with forty cats and dogs. Brando visited her and made her promise that if she ever decided to leave the island, she would sell it to him.

Otherwise, the experience of being on Tahiti was an absolute nightmare "and marked the pinnacle of Brando's self-indulgence," Peter Manso writes. *Mutiny* was plagued by difficulties, by endless delays caused by tropical storms, badly scouted locations, illnesses and deaths in the company. There were constant disagreements between the star and the first director, Sir Carol Reed. He was either fired or quit midway through the production, after accusing Brando of being "lazy and frivolous." He was replaced by Lewis Milestone, a grizzled veteran who'd directed classics like *All Quiet on the Western Front*. He fought with Brando, whose weight ballooned from 170 to 210 pounds, necessitating special lighting and constant costume adjustments. The two men kept arguing over the script. There were twenty-seven versions, and none of them ever had an ending. As time went on, Brando became more and more impossible, often stalking off the set mid-scene. The other stars of the picture, Richard Harris and Trevor Howard, found him "unprofessional and absolutely ridiculous. He could drive a saint to hell in a dogsled," Howard said.

Just before the picture wrapped, Milestone quit, and George Seaton shot the final sequence, Christian's death scene. For that scene Brando insisted on lying on a bed of ice to re-create his mother's death throes.

Finally, in October 1961, a mass of film was put together in the MGM editing rooms. But there was still no ending to the movie. All the writers struggled to find one until the following year, when director-writer Billy Wilder happened to come up with one. Brando agreed with it, and it was filmed.

By that time *Mutiny* had cost twenty million dollars, with another seven million for prints and advertising. MGM, close to bankruptcy, put all the blame on Brando, who had been exceedingly difficult, although other problems, such as an incomplete script and badly scouted locations, had contributed to *Mutiny*'s astronomical losses. But MGM planted disparaging stories about Brando in the press, and he threatened to bring legal action against it unless it stopped. He also filed a five-million-dollar suit against the Curtis Publishing Company for libeling him in a *Saturday Evening Post* article entitled "How Brando Broke the Budget in a Remake of *Mutiny on the Bounty*."

Hollywood had never liked or approved of Marlon Brando. He was too eccentric, too unruly. For a while his huge box-office successes and his Oscar kept everybody quiet, but the sheer volume of bad publicity was making him the subject of ridicule. His behavior, his wild reputation, not his artistry, were being reviewed. He was fallible now, and he knew it. "They start out by seducing you, and then they end up pissing on you," he said.

When *Mutiny* was finally released, critics lambasted the movie. *Time* magazine called it "sentimental bilge." However, Richard Schickel, in his biography of Brando, maintains that Fletcher Christian is a brave, original creation, one of Brando's most intriguing performances: "delicious, wonderful—comic and socially acute. And of a piece." If the rest of the cast had been up to him, this version of *Mutiny* could have turned into a cult film instead of a joke.

At this point Brando's career was sinking, and Anna Kashfi's irrational behavior was driving him crazy. She could not be controlled. She was drinking; she was on drugs; she had fits of elation and wild depression and would come at him with a knife. She was also diagnosed as an epileptic, and later she attempted suicide. There were constant custody battles; Brando was deeply worried about little Christian.

That wasn't all. Brando had financial obligations to Movita and their son, Miko, and daughter, Rebecca, and he was soon to have a child by Tarita. His father's sloppy financial planning had left him without much real capital or income from investments. He was worried about his children's future. He had other people dependent on him too, other girlfriends and friends and relatives. Marlon continued to be overly generous to a lot of people, Pat Cox said.

Jay Kanter (no longer his agent, now a movie executive) concocted the following deal, in which Universal would buy Pennebaker for a reported one million dollars and back its next production, *The Ugly American*, which Brando had long wanted to star in. A thinly disguised tract on the failure of American foreign policy in Southeast Asia, the movie itself, based on the best-selling book by Eugene Burdick and William J. Lederer, was a failure despite Brando's intensive publicity campaign.

The rest of the deal was this: He committed himself to star in a certain number of films for Universal at $270,000 apiece, a real comedown after he'd received $1 million for *The Fugitive*

Kind. There would be terrible consequences for him, but he needed the money, so he agreed to it.

In the next ten years he made seventeen movies, five for Universal, and the rest independent. A lot of them were movies he didn't really want to make, but he was so financially strapped that he had to. Among them are the abysmal *Bedtime Story*, a sorry attempt at a comedy that Brando genuinely enjoyed doing, because his costar David Niven constantly made him laugh; a so-called spy thriller, *Morituri*, with Yul Brynner; *The Appaloosa*, a Mexican western in which his ritual punishment consists of being dragged through a rocky stream by a galloping horse; and a 1930s type of farce, *The Countess of Hong Kong*, which was directed by Charlie Chaplin. Among Brando's memories were Chaplin's sadistic treatment of his son Sydney—"He was vicious to him"—and the "bad breath" of his costar, Sophia Loren.

Suffice it to say that in each of these movies there were flashes of the old Brando brilliance, and you see him trying to achieve the arc of a character. But overall he seemed distant, professional but uninspired, and these films did nothing at the box office. He became increasingly depressed, and he gained a lot of weight.

He was feeling especially lousy when he and Elia Kazan visited Clifford Odets, who was dying of pancreatic cancer in Cedars of Lebanon Hospital, in August 1961. After the two men moved out into the waiting room, Brando suddenly muttered, "Here I am, a balding, middle-aged failure....I feel a fraud when I act....I've tried everything...fucking, drinking, work. None of them mean anything. Why can't we be like—like the Tahitians?"

He wanted to do something worthwhile, something that would make a difference. So he went to Northeast India, where the Bihar famine was making headlines around the world, and he tried to make a documentary with his own money about UNICEF's emergency food program. The suffering he filmed was devastating: emaciated children, starving men and women who were denied food because they were "untouchables." The hospital rooms he visited were gray with flies. On his last day he watched a child die in front of him from malnutrition, and he put down his camera and cried. When he returned to the United States, he showed his film to Jack Valenti, then President Lyndon Johnson's special assistant. Valenti assured him the president would see the film, but that was the last Brando heard from him. He showed the film to many important people in Hollywood, but nobody seemed interested; he could not get the film on TV. Later UNICEF did use portions of it for fund-raising.

Meanwhile he kept looking for another Kazan, another director who understood the kind of values he placed on acting, story, and character. He thought he'd found one in Arthur Penn, also a member of the Actors Studio and already famous in the New York theater for his superb productions of *Two for the Seesaw* and *The Miracle Worker*.

In the summer of 1965, while Watts was burning and the two of them were working together with Sammy Davis, Jr., in the civil rights struggle, Penn directed Brando in a film called *The Chase*, with a screenplay by Lillian Hellman. The plot exploited the hysterical vision that Texans had been con-spiring to kill JFK. Brando plays a paunchy liberal sheriff who attempts to keep a lid on the unruly passions of his reactionary cowpoke town. The cast surrounding him were mostly members of the Actors Studio—Jane Fonda, Robert Redford, Robert Duvall, and Janice Rule—as well as Angie Dickinson, who plays his wife. Everyone was in awe and excited about working with Brando.

Brando, for his part, was determined to reverse the damage done to his reputation by *Mutiny*. "It was a delight to watch him sort of hunker down on the set," Arthur Penn told Richard Schickel. "He'd slowly make it his own—move this around here, move that around there, and pretty soon it would be his place, his environment. And he'd improvise constantly, change the rhythm and inflection of his lines. Marlon is the consummate improvisor. It is really his way to 'get' the character."

He helped stage the savage fight scene where the sheriff is beaten on his way to rescue Robert Redford from the lynch mob. For his makeup, "Marlon drenched his face with blood and kept a cigar stuffed in his mouth all the while he was being pummeled almost to death," an observer said. Brando's obses-sion with the beating incident made sense, because he was reversing his character's action. Instead of restoring order to his lawless town, "the sheriff is gonna stagger away from it."

In the evenings after filming, there were noisy parties and fund-raisers for the Congress of Racial Equality (CORE) at Penn's home (he was renting Sammy Davis, Jr.'s house in Beverly Hills). Political activism dominated Hollywood in the mid-1960s, and Brando was at the forefront. He would make a big impression when he appeared at a huge civil rights march in Mississippi led by James Meredith, Martin Luther King, Jr., and Stokely Carmichael.

Initially he seemed pleased with *The Chase*. Then its producer, Sam Spiegel, came on the set and began tinkering with the script and upping the quotient for violence, "in the interest of big box office," he said. Brando got disgusted and was heard to say, "If they're going to be stupid fucks, I'll take the money and do my job, and that's it." Ultimately Spiegel broke his contract with Penn and took the negative to London, where the film was edited with no directorial supervision, and "all the great improvisations were cut," Penn said in an interview.

The first New York screening of *The Chase* was an absolute disaster, Richard Schickel says, with the audience hooting and hollering and talking back to the screen. Today, decades later, the movie is being reevaluated, along with some of Brando's other work that was not accepted by the critics at the time.

During the 1960s Brando was proud of only one performance, the repressed homosexual Major Weldon Penderton in Carson McCullers's gothic tale *Reflections in a Golden Eye*, which John Huston directed in 1967, and in which Brando pursued a variation on what Schickel calls his great theme of "moving toward an acceptance of a painful truth about himself." Elizabeth Taylor costarred, along with Julie Harris. The story revolves around couples who are all "trying to escape from the sexual closets in which they are entrapped."

Brando is remarkable, from his "strangled southern accent to his plastered-down hair" and immaculate uniform. He's like "a little boy playing soldier." At one point he salutes his reflection in the mirror.

There's a terrifying scene in which his wife's stallion runs away with him through the woods, as he is attempting to catch a glimpse of the soldier he's obsessed with, who is nude in a clearing. When Brando is thrown, he is so humiliated that he beats the horse almost to death and then collapses in tears. "So the sequence becomes a confrontation with his imperfect primal self, the self that all his posturings cannot hide," Schickel writes.

Throughout the movie Brando takes risks, but after his character suddenly realizes what he wants sexually, he takes even more risks as an actor. He pouts; he blubbers; he pats cold cream on his face like a teenage girl as he awaits the gentleman caller, the soldier he longs for, who turns out to be lusting for his wife instead of him.

It was "almost as if he was exploring his own sexuality," his costar Julie Harris said, "yet his work was so beautiful and so pure that there was no explaining where it came from. He still didn't love acting, he didn't love the theater and he didn't respect his own talent, but his gift was so great he couldn't defile it. He could put on pounds, he could say it was all shit, but he still couldn't destroy it."

John Huston believed that *Reflections* was one of the finest films he ever made, but the public was turned off by the themes of impotence, homosexuality, and psychological torment. The movie was a box-office failure after it opened in 1967. One wonders if Brando was embittered when his astonishing performance went unnoticed.

His next picture was the truly dreadful *Candy,* a pornographic spoof by Terry Southern, directed by Christian Marquand, in which Brando plays a zany Indian guru. As for *The Night of the Following Day,* a spy thriller, Brando mocked, "This movie makes as much sense as a rat fucking a grapefruit." He was increasingly filled with anger and self-contempt. In fact around this time he was quoted as saying, "Acting is a bum's life. It leads to perfect self-indulgence. You get paid for doing nothing and it adds up to nothing."

After each movie he'd disappear to his atoll near Tahiti in French Polynesia, the only place he wanted to be, "the only place I have ever known happiness," he says. In 1967 he had purchased the atoll, Tetiaroa, for $270,000, and it seemed to offer the perfect escape from all his problems: his unending custody battles, his widely publicized affairs. He lived there in a simple thatched-roof hut, just one large room with a double bed covered with mosquito netting, a picture of his mother nearby.

He had grandiose plans: He wanted to create a think tank, a colony where artists, scientists, and literary folk could come and trade opinions and ideas in order to make the world a better place. He would pour millions of dollars into Tetiaroa for environmental projects. He was worried about a nuclear holocaust wiping out much of civilization, and he saw the place as a haven for his family and his children. He wanted more than anything to make the island self-sufficient. He eventually built a hotel and an airstrip and tried to promote the atoll as a tourist attraction. But his efforts to civilize and improve Tetiaroa were doomed, one of his biographers said, by his "inattention, unreal expectations, and insensitivity to the clash of cultures."

13

BRANDO FACED A WHOLE new set of variables in 1968. Hollywood was convulsed again, this time by a recession and by Paramount's being bought by Gulf & Western, which started the conglomerate trend. It was also a watershed year of political unrest and turmoil in America: The country still appeared to be reeling from the effects of John F. Kennedy's assassination in Dallas; there were protests against the war in Vietnam and riots at Columbia University.

By that time Brando was one of the most important activists in Hollywood, joining Harry Belafonte, Burt Lancaster, and Sidney Poitier in raising money for CORE and for Martin Luther King. Using his fame as a political tool, Brando appeared on TV and radio whenever he could, speaking out against atrocities leveled at southern blacks. He'd become so preoccupied by the threat of racial violence he was thinking of giving up acting entirely to devote himself to civil rights.

He turned down Kazan's *The Arrangement* and agreed to do *Burn!* only because he believed the movie would have "appropriate significance." It was about the making and breaking of a peasant revolutionary in a Caribbean country, and he was to play an eighteenth-century agent provocateur from England who is sent to foment insurrection. What really excited him was that it would be directed by Gillo Pontecorvo, whose earlier movie *Battle of Algiers,* shot with handheld cameras and cast with nonactors, was considered a textbook on revolution by both black and white leftists.

Brando approached *Burn!* as he approached any project that intrigued him: He started to do research, as he had with the motorcycle gang, as he had when he traveled around Mexico for *Zapata,* as he had when he was evolving into Stanley Kowalski and used to sit in the phone booth in Times Square watching the passing parade.

In this instance he wanted to psych out revolutionaries, and who better than the Black Panthers? They were a controversial militant political party in Oakland that, armed with law-books and guns, patrolled the ghetto, fighting police brutality and making sure that their constitutional rights were respected.

Several members of the usually secretive group agreed to meet Brando because "I had always admired Marlon from the time I was sixteen and saw *The Wild One,*" Panther leader Bobby Seale told Peter Manso. Seale said he also identified with his character in *Waterfront.* "I knew...he had this rebellious streak in him, too....I was extremely receptive to him coming up to see us."

On a foggy afternoon in February, Brando met with the Panthers at Eldridge Cleaver's Haight-Ashbury apartment in San Francisco. Also present were Kathleen Cleaver, Bobby Seale, and the slender seventeen-year-old Bobby Hutton, the

Panthers' secretary, who made a strong impression on Brando because he seemed to have so much dignity.

Brando writes of this meeting, "We talked till almost four A.M., and I learned a great deal about a variety of subjects, but especially about the day-to-day experiences of being a black man in Oakland—of being stopped and searched by policemen simply because he was black, of being degraded, belittled and called 'nigger' by cops, of applying for a job and seeing in the eyes of employers that as soon as he entered their doors the job no longer existed."

Kathleen Cleaver recalls that "Brando couldn't take his eyes off Eldridge. It was as if he was just glued to him, trying to absorb everything about him all at once." Cleaver, whose best-selling book *Soul on Ice* had made him something of a celebrity, was acting president of the Panthers, since their elected president, Huey Newton, was in jail on a murder charge.

Near the end of their conversation (which was very "intense," Seale remembers), Brando produced the *Burn!* script and explained that he was going to make this movie but needed to understand "just how real revolutionaries felt—how they reacted to the white power structure, because he, Brando, was going to be playing the white oppressor. He started to ask questions like 'What makes you go out and take a chance you may get killed?'" He seemed more interested in understanding how they felt about being revolutionaries than in hearing about the Panthers' agenda on violence and their position on self-defense.

Before he was driven back to the airport, Brando asked Cleaver to be a consultant on the *Burn!* film, but Cleaver ended up saying no. Even so, they kept in touch with each other from then on, and Brando gave the Panthers money. When more Panthers were "busted," he paid for bail, Seale told Manso. During the spring of 1968 Brando's home at the top of Mulholland Drive became a hangout for many left-wing activists, like novelist James Baldwin and actress Jean Seberg.

On April 4, 1968, thirty-nine-year-old civil rights leader Martin Luther King, Jr., was assassinated in Memphis. Brando watched the news on TV, horrified as Tennessee's governor, Buford Ellington, ordered four thousand National Guard troops into Memphis to keep order, and a curfew was imposed, since 40 percent of the city's population was black.

Bobby Seale phoned and asked for help in getting to King's funeral in Atlanta. Brando sent him plane tickets and hotel reservations, not just for himself but also for two other Panthers.

After the funeral Huey Newton and Seale came to Brando's hotel suite, where a contingent of Hollywood stars and others had gathered to share their grief. Among them were Sammy Davis, Jr., Harry Belafonte, James Baldwin, Sidney Poitier, and Tony Franciosa.

By then America's blacks, enraged by King's murder, were rioting in various cities—Cincinnati, Chicago, and Baltimore—and parts of Washington, D.C., were nothing but smoking rubble. The Panthers were incensed by what was happening and shouted that they wanted to take up their guns. Franciosa recalls that one of them turned to Brando and asked, "What would you do?" and Brando told them quietly, "I would not take up any guns." Franciosa added, "Marlon didn't talk at them but with them. He was honestly trying to allay their fears. He wanted to unify instead of separate."

Seale was very depressed. He wasn't mourning just King but also Bobby Hutton, the seventeen-year-old secretary of the Black Panthers, who'd been shot by police in a gun battle outside Panther headquarters two nights after the King murder. The house caught fire, and when Hutton walked outside, the police shot him. Eldridge Cleaver and eight others were wounded.

On April 12, 1968, Brando, neatly dressed in a suit and tie, attended Hutton's funeral in Oakland, which was widely covered by the media. Then he appeared at a rally of nearly two thousand mourners near the county jail where Huey Newton was being held for murdering a policeman. Brando stood on a flatbed truck and told the throng that Bobby Hutton "could be my son." Then he added, "The preacher said that the white man can't cool it because he has never dug it. I am trying to dig it, and that's why I'm here. You've been listening to white people for four hundred years, and they haven't done a thing. Now I'm going to begin right now informing white people what they don't know." He promised that he would raise money and make the public aware of what the police had been doing.

As he was speaking, he noticed that James Farmer, head of the Congress of Racial Equality, was looking at him with hatred in his eyes. "They told me that he despised me because I was just another knee-jerk white liberal to him," Brando writes in his autobiography. "At Bobby Hutton's funeral, I began to sense why Jim Farmer had looked at me that way and to understand—as I have at other moments in my life in other places when I was among people I wanted to help—that I was an outsider." Rap Brown told Brando essentially the same thing: that he was poking his nose in a world he didn't know and didn't belong in, and to get out.

But comedian activist Dick Gregory recalled, "Marlon's participation in the civil rights movement was crucial, especially when he demonstrated in the deep South." Brando had gone to Gadsden, Alabama, where there had been vicious clashes between blacks and the law. He'd spoken in black homes and in black churches, always with authority and gentleness. Gregory continued, "In the South black folks had been dominated by powerful white folks, so when Marlon came in, it was like telling the black folks, 'White folks say it's okay.' I mean this was Brando. Nobody in the history of the movement made a difference like that."

At the end of May, Brando abruptly withdrew his support from the Panthers after Eldridge Cleaver published a manifesto that said in part that true revolutionaries should be willing to kill their parents in order to achieve their goals. He never publicly denounced the Panthers, but he did go on *The Tonight Show* to tell Johnny Carson that since King's assassination, he, Barbra Streisand, Paul Newman, and Drew Pearson were pledging 1 percent of their earnings from then on to the Southern Christian Leadership Conference. Carson announced he would do the same.

That summer, after Robert Kennedy's murder, Brando distanced himself from political activism almost entirely. He was too preoccupied by his complicated private life. Movita had filed for divorce, and he had to handle that along with his terrible problems with Kashfi and the fact that his son Christian was "tense, tearful, and terrorized, unable to pay attention or relate well to adults."

Then there was the necessity of resuming his career to film *Burn!* Brando and the cast and crew were to suffer through six months of sweltering heat on location in Cartagena, Colombia, where the temperature rose to 105 degrees. Originally he had been excited about making *Burn!*, but he and director Pontecorvo fought angrily over the uncompleted script and over the supposed mistreatment of the huge native cast (Brando was sure they were being fed tainted food). After Pontecorvo insisted he do forty takes of a scene in which he stood in the hot sun while a sugarcane field burned behind him, Brando left Cartagena and flew back to Los Angeles. The production shut down for months while various lawyers fought, and Alberto Grimaldi, the producer, sued Brando for $750,000.

The movie was completed in a nontropical third world country, Morocco, and when it was shown in theaters in 1969, at least twenty minutes of the director's cut were missing. The film looks beautiful but makes very little sense. Even so, today Brando maintains he gives his greatest performance in *Burn!*, and he says that aside from Kazan and Bertolucci, "Pontecorvo is the greatest director I ever worked with."

14

BRANDO REMAINED HAUNTED BY his parents. Memories of the songs his mother taught him wafted through his head, and he continued to obsess about his father, even though Senior had died in 1965. He told Pat Cox how he'd gone back to Illinois to "scatter Pop's ashes" on the family farm, and he'd been in the kitchen, sort of shaking the box of ashes, when he'd heard a dull rattle and realized that tiny pieces of some of Pop's bones were still in the box. He didn't want "animals gnawing on any part of that mean carcass," so at dusk he plodded out into the field, and as if he were sowing seeds, he sprinkled the ashes very gently onto the earth.

He writes in his autobiography that after his father died, he had a dream about him: "I had a vision of him walking down a sidewalk away from me, then turning around to look at me, a slump-shouldered Willy Loman with a faint smile on his face. When he got to the edge of eternity, he stopped and looked back again, turned halfway toward me, and, with his eyes downcast, said: *I did the best I could, kid.* He turned away again, and I knew he was looking for my mother."

But for a long time after his death, Brando couldn't stop hating his father. "I used to think, 'God, just give him to me alive for eight seconds; that's all I want...because I want to break his jaw.' I wanted to smash his face and watch him spit out his teeth. I wanted to kick his balls into his throat. I wanted to rip his ears off and eat them in front of him. I wanted to separate his larynx from his body and shove it in his stomach." For a long time Brando refused to give up the fantasy of revenge.

Pat Cox feels that "Marlon's hatred of his father fueled his huge talent. The hatred burned night and day. It erupted in *Streetcar* and Waterfront and *Last Tango*. His best movies are about anger—the control and display of anger, as well as anger's indulgence."

But with time he began to realize that he would never be free until he eradicated these feelings. With time, he also saw "a little of him in me....He was a very angry man, as I was for most of my life." Ultimately he realized that he would have to forgive his father for all his slights and put-downs and psychological brutality if he were ever going to be able to get on with his life.

By the start of 1970 Brando was virtually unemployable. He was hugely overweight and constantly depressed. He'd made ten box-office fiascos, and he had a reputation for being troublesome and uncooperative. He remained immersed in court battles with Kashfi, as well as other lawsuits, including one with three Oakland policemen stemming from remarks he'd made on *The Joey Bishop Show* about the Bobby Hutton case in 1968.

Brando had so little money he was forced to accept a paltry fifty thousand dollars to star in a low-budget horror movie titled *The Nightcomers,* to be shot in England the following year. He would be playing an Irish gamekeeper, a hypnotic storyteller, who was able to dominate little children with his macabre tales.

Months before, Mario Puzo had sent him the galleys of his book *The Godfather,* the epic story of an American crime family. It went on to be one of the biggest best-sellers ever; the book was being developed into a movie by Paramount, with Puzo writing the script. Although he still hadn't read it, Brando called to thank him for the book, and Puzo said he had always pictured him as Don Corleone in the movie version. With that, Brando chuckled wanly and said he doubted Paramount would ever hire him.

However, weeks later, when the mercurial thirty-one-year-old Francis Ford Coppola was signed on to direct and to help Puzo rewrite the script, he too thought of Brando for the aging Mafia don. The part, although not the largest in the movie, dominates the narrative, and it needed an actor of exceptional presence to play it. The only other actors Coppola considered for the part were Laurence Olivier and George C. Scott. Subsequently, *Godfather* producer Al Ruddy and Coppola contacted Brando and persuaded him to read not only the novel but the rough draft of the screenplay. Brando said he doubted he could play an Italian gangster. He sounded so negative they were astonished when three days later he not only agreed to play the part but seemed quite enthusiastic about it, saying that the movie reflected something metaphorical about cor-

Brando in *The Godfather* and as aging expatriate Paul in *Last Tango in Paris*, between them, critic Foster Hirsch said, they span the poles of his genius: "The first is his greatest performance, the second his most unsparing act of self-revelation."

porate mentality. To him, the gangsters parodied establishment values.

Now Ruddy and Coppola had to convince Paramount executives that Brando should play the Godfather. They met with Stanley Jaffe, president of the studio, and Robert Evans, chief of production. Both men ridiculed the idea of Brando, until Coppola pleaded his case in bravura style. He gave a ten-minute oration, declaring that Brando had such a mythic relationship with the public and with other actors that his presence would elevate the film. The director ended his speech by collapsing on the floor and hyperventilating until the executives agreed, but only on the conditions that Brando would accept fifty thousand dollars as salary, that a bond would be posted to be used in case he "misbehaved," and that he had to do a screen test.

Ruddy and Coppola left the meeting wondering how they could ask Oscar winner Marlon Brando to take a screen test. Then Coppola thought up a way. He would tell the forty-seven-year-old Brando he wanted to photograph him in makeup to test whether he could really pass for a sixty-five-year-old Italian man.

Privately Brando was already excited about the project. He'd never before been able to disguise himself totally, or his despised movie star persona for that matter. This part would permit him to hide completely, as he had seen his idol Paul Muni do.

Days after the meeting with Paramount brass, Coppola arrived at Brando's Mulholland Drive home with a videocam operator and an actor, Salvatore Corsitto, who was told to wait outside in the garden. The director went into the house and started the camera rolling. Coppola told his biographer Michael Schumacher: "In my video you see Brando coming out of his bedroom with his long blond hair in a ponytail. He is dressed in a Japanese kimono. You see him roll up his hair in a bun and blacken it with shoe polish, talking all the time about what he's doing. You see him rolling up Kleenex and stuffing it into his mouth. He'd decided that the Godfather had been shot in the throat at one time, so he starts to speak funny. Then he takes a jacket and rolls back the collar the way these Mafia guys do....Then I give him a Toscani cigar."

Coppola also set out a plate of apples and cheese on a table, along with a tiny espresso cup, props for Brando to work with.

The telephone rang, and as he began improvising a conversation, Coppola called in Corsitto and introduced him as one of the don's minions. Brando immediately fell into the character of Don Corleone, and the two actors ad-libbed a little scene. When they replayed the tape on the monitor, Brando was delighted with what he saw. "It's the face of a bulldog," he said, "mean-looking but warm underneath."

Several months passed. Brando was in London shooting *The Nightcomers* when he heard that he would star as the Godfather. From then on he worked with more enthusiasm than he had shown in a long time. "A marvelous complex muddled anarchistic amazing talent," his costar Stephanie Beacham wrote in her diary. In fact, Brando's performance as the sadistic Irish gamekeeper is alive and bursting with sexual energy, although nobody noticed: the movie did nothing after it opened. Within two years he was to explore that same kind of sexual darkness in *Last Tango in Paris*.

Meanwhile, in January 1971, Coppola flew to London to confer with him about how the don should be played. He brought research he thought would trigger his imagination: news stories on Mafia leaders, tape recordings of gangster Frank Costello at the Kefauver crime hearings. Brando was taken by Costello's high-pitched voice and eventually copied it for *The Godfather*. Coppola told him, "The Godfather could be played as a sweet little old man. Powerful people don't need to shout."

"Before we started, I thought Marlon was this strange, moody titan, but he turned out to be very simple, direct," Coppola said later. "He was very tactile. He likes to touch you. He likes to be dealt with honestly. Likes to feel he's listened to, and told 'No' when his idea is stupid, and 'Yes' when it's good. I avoided intellectual discussions, tried to make him feel like he wouldn't be taken advantage of."

That weekend in London the young bearded director couldn't stop pouring out his troubles. A compulsive self-dramatist, he quickly drew Brando into the operatic turmoil of his life and career. He'd started off in life as a bedridden Italian kid with polio, who kept himself entertained by playing with puppets. He really didn't want to do *Godfather*, he said, but he needed the money to pursue his dreams. Brando saw him as a romantic and an idealist, as he had once been. He understood why Coppola was in such an agitated state. He was fighting to get a bigger budget for *Godfather*, he told Brando. He was fighting to get Al Pacino for Michael, instead of Warren Beatty. Once during that weekend, he shattered the phone to pieces after speaking to Robert Evans, who had already announced that he had cast Beatty in the role. At one point Brando phoned Evans and told him the role of Michael required "a brooder," that Pacino's elegant minimalism would work; he needed room to develop the character. Brando's assurances helped Pacino land the role.

Before the weekend in London was over, Brando was carrying trays of food to the young director's desk while Coppola tried to bat out another scene in the unfinished *Godfather* screenplay, and then he would stop and read it out loud. He had done only four movies. None of them had been especially successful, he said, and he was scared.

There were other problems. The Mafia was applying pressure on Paramount through the Italian-American Civil Rights League; there were bomb threats and other intimidations, until producer Al Ruddy promised never to use the words "Mafia" or "Cosa Nostra." He also had to hire people recommended by the league to work on the production.

Meanwhile Brando began preparing for his part with a dedication that seemed contrary to his public contempt for acting. Before the shoot began, he arranged to have a ritualistic "family" dinner in New Jersey with a mobster dynasty, very rich, very powerful, very private. "About forty people were there," says Phil Rhodes, who accompanied Brando. "Marlon sat with them," eating their excellent pasta, drinking their fine wines, listening as they spoke Italian half the time. He noted how polite they were, how gracious. During the evening they brought him their babies to kiss, and he met with their cousins and old aunts. He noted their preoccupation with food, and he noted as well that the women seemed to be controlled and indulged and dependent. He was surprised at the depth of passion and genuine love this family of criminals seemed to have for one another.

Shooting of the movie began in October 1971, down on Mulberry Street, and continued all over Manhattan and Staten Island. The first few weeks Coppola had a rough time. He had to reshoot and rewrite scenes because he realized the original drafts weren't working. He had constant arguments about lighting and blocking with cinematographer Gordon Willis, who was favoring a dark, stylized look.

Rumors circulated that Coppola was going to be fired and replaced by Elia Kazan. A friend advised him to resign. Brando said, "If you fire Francis, I'll walk off the picture." Then Coppola won the Academy Award for the screenplay for *Patton,* and he fired everybody who'd questioned his authority, and somehow the film continued.

He had to rewrite dialogue a lot, even on the set. Then the atmosphere got tense since Brando always refused to memorize his new lines. He had cue cards all over the place, pasted on desks, on the fruit in the bowl on Don Corleone's table; sometimes he wrote his lines on the back of his hand or on his sleeve. Others in the cast found it unsettling, too, but when Coppola confronted him about it, Brando denied it was memory loss or failure to concentrate. He maintained he'd done the same thing in *Waterfront.* "Real people don't know what they're going to say. Their words often come as a surprise. That's the way it should be in a movie."

Coppola bent over backward to incorporate suggestions from Brando, even in the midst of shooting a scene. "I could understand why he had this crazy reputation, because his ideas were often so bizarre. But without exception, every one of his ideas I used turned out to be a terrific moment." As when Brando thought of slapping Johnny Fontane, the singer, "to bring him to his senses"; as when, in the middle of the line "After all, we're not murderers, no matter what the undertakers say," he inhales the fragrance of a rose.

The other actors in the cast—Al Pacino, Robert Duvall, James Caan—were in awe of him. "In a sense, Marlon had created these guys," producer Al Ruddy told Charles Higham. The night before they started shooting, Coppola gathered everybody at a big Italian restaurant for a dinner meeting, with Marlon at the head of the table. "They all stood frozen when they first met him, and then he cracked a joke. Marlon's lack of bullshit relaxed everybody."

At the dinner Brando debated with Coppola whether to show the don's evil side or good side. He didn't want to play him as a cliché gangster like Eddie Robinson; he saw him as a man of substance and of tradition.

Dick Smith and Phil Rhodes had created the Godfather look by devising a plastic triangular mouthpiece to push out the cheeks. Then the skin of Brando's face was painted with latex rubber and allowed to dry. When the skin relaxed under the rubber, it created a network of lines and wrinkles. Weights were put in his shoes to make him walk heavily. He wore earplugs, which muffled what the actors were saying, so he had to strain to hear them. He'd come out of his dressing room in the morning and plod over to a chair, stooped and weary-eyed and aging. Crew members would actually step aside as if in deference.

He totally inhabited the role. When they weren't in a scene,

Al Pacino, Diane Keaton, and James Caan would stand on the sidelines, watching him work. He was constantly inventing. Even in disguise he was giving a pure Method performance; a great actor was working behind this masquerade.

While they were shooting at Filmways Studio on 127th Street, Brando discovered a mangy old gray cat prowling the area. He cradled the cat on his lap during all the scenes that showed him meeting with key gangsters from around the country. He would stroke the cat lovingly as he talked about murder. "It was an incredible juxtaposition of terror and gentleness," Brando biographer Bob Thomas said.

Between takes he'd relax and joke with the crew, but he always remained in character. He never stopped speaking in the gravelly, wheezy croak he'd developed for the don.

Maybe this is the moment to discuss Brando's voice, because he is really a master of vocal disguise and should be given credit for it. (What doesn't count are the hundreds of times he's disguised his voice on the phone to friends and strangers. He's still doing it today, as he operates his ham radio and talks to people all over the world.) But his vocal trickery began when he was a young actor in New York, imitating people he'd hear on the streets.

The voice audiences still recognize or connect with him is Stanley Kowalski's, the voice he is most famous for, the voice of the American working-class male, guttural, mocking, slightly high-pitched. It is just one of his many vocal masks. Foster Hirsch, in his book *Acting Hollywood Style,* comments that "Brando's accents have been largely imagined as opposed to realistic." As Napoleon in *Désirée,* he used clipped British tones. His Marc Antony is pure general American, which shows that both Stanley and Terry Malloy are skillful masquerades. Then there is his Japanese con man Sakini in *Teahouse of the August Moon,* which is a comic invention, as is his Indian guru in Terry Southern's *Candy.* For *The Chase* and Reflections in a Golden Eye, Brando rolls out a lush southern drawl, and for the Nazi in *Young Lions,* it's German. His Don Corleone had a raspy, fragile vocal pattern, cracking with age and catarrh.

As he filmed *Godfather,* he was really enjoying himself. He got a big kick out of Jimmy Caan's mooning him as he drove past in his limousine after work, so Brando mooned back. After the wedding feast was filmed, everybody applauded and laughed when Caan and Duvall presented him with a silver belt buckle emblazoned with "Mighty Moon Champion."

There was more applause in the scene in which he was cut down by bullets on Mott Street. A huge crowd gathered to watch, including some real-life dons, and after Brando was wounded by a hail of bullets and collapsed against the hood of a car, the crowd cheered and yelled. With that, Brando rose and made a grand bow, like an opera singer. He was so relaxed that after the scene was over, he lay down on the street and fell asleep. In the evenings, he kept to himself, going back to his hotel, the Elysee on East Fifty-fourth Street, and seeing only Phil and Marie Rhodes and his secretary, Alice Marchak.

Brando's scenes in *The Godfather* took six weeks to shoot. Coppola was worried about his last scene, between Don Corleone and his son Michael, which Robert Towne was rewriting. Brando thought the scene made the Godfather too manipulative toward Michael. At one point Coppola, Towne, and Pacino met in Brando's dressing room, and they all contributed their thoughts. But Brando offered the key: "Just once I'd like to hear Don Corleone express himself well."

The next morning Towne brought the new dialogue to Brando and read it to him. Brando liked it. The scene depicted the succession of power, with the elder Corleone reminding the son of duties that needed to be performed. Michael told him he had done the necessary things. Then the don asked him about Michael's son, and Michael said his son was already reading the funnies.

Brando told Towne, "I'd like to repeat that line, 'He reads the funnies.'" Again, a Brando detail. It added to the scene, emphasizing the grandfather's pride and an old man's decline. He performed the scene with Pacino, reading the lines scrawled on blackboards placed behind the cameras.

Then came the final scene, the Godfather's death. He was supposed to collapse of a heart attack after playing in the garden with his grandson.

The scene wasn't going well. The actor cast as the grandson wasn't reacting. So Coppola asked Brando for help, and he suggested a trick Phil Rhodes had shown him that they'd both done with their kids, cutting fangs out of orange rind and putting them under his lip to make himself resemble a movie monster. The little boy responded immediately, and then Don Corleone, the gentle old man who in real life had indeed been a monster, toppled over dead in the garden.

Up until the last minute Coppola was sure he'd made a flop. He said to somebody, after seeing the rough cut, "I failed. I took a pulpy, salacious novel and turned it into a movie about a bunch of guys sitting in a dark room talking."

Paramount eventually announced that *The Godfather* had made more money than any film in history up to that time. Brando was pleased, but he had not forgotten the humiliating conditions under which he had been given the role of Don Corleone, so he held out for so much money when *The Godfather II* was made that they ended up rewriting the script so he would not be in it. Then when Robert Evans asked him to play Jay Gatsby opposite his wife, Ali MacGraw, in a remake of *The Great Gatsby,* Brando took over the negotiations himself and again asked for so much money the deal fell through.

The powerful entertainment lawyer Norman Garey was to negotiate most of his future deals, including *Superman* and The Missouri Breaks, which were so lucrative and far-reaching that Brando finally became a very wealthy man.

15

THE GODFATHER MARKED Brando's comeback, but there is no simple explanation for the splendid zenith of *Last Tango in Paris*—just a series of coincidences and perfect timing: the right phone call from an old friend, Luigi Luraschi, who headed Paramount's Rome office and who told him that director Bernardo Bertolucci had an intriguing idea for a movie. Brando's trusted secretary, Alice Marchak, urged him to check out the idea.

Bertolucci's movie came at a personal and career crossroads for Brando, and maybe he knew that. It ended up being his preeminent film, certainly the most radical, and his work in it stands apart from everything else he had done, "where his full art is realized," Pauline Kael wrote in *The New Yorker*. "Intuitive, rapt, princely, on the screen Brando is our genius, just as surely as Norman Mailer is our genius in literature."

Bertolucci, then thirty-one, recalls his first meeting with Brando at the Hôtel Raphäl in Paris in the spring of 1971. "He just sat and looked at me for fifteen minutes without speaking." The director felt shy and in awe of Brando; he had first seen him in the movies as Zapata when he was a kid. "And then Marlon began talking in sweet Tahitian French." Bertolucci would say he learned to speak English from Marlon Brando, who mumbles a lot, "which is why nobody understands me."

The following day, at Brando's request, Bertolucci screened his latest film, *The Conformist,* starring Dominique Sanda and Jean-Paul Trintignant (whom he had originally wanted for *Tango*). Set in 1930s Fascist Italy, the story is about an upper-class follower of Mussolini; the production had been highly praised for its sensuous texture and velvety operatic style. After it was over, Brando nodded in approval. He added that a friend whose judgment he really respected had insisted he see the film. Bertolucci learned that the friend was an elegant Chinese lady named Anita Kong, one of Brando's longtime lovers. She had seen it seven times.

Then Brando asked, "What's your idea for me?" and Bertolucci described the part he envisioned for him, that of Paul, an American expatriate living in Paris, middle-aged, despairing, whose French wife, Rose, has just inexplicably committed suicide in the fleabag hotel she owns. By chance Paul runs into a free-spirited young woman, Jeanne, in the empty apartment they're both thinking of renting. He abruptly seduces her, rents the apartment, and what follows is a doomed "sex-only" affair that lasts for three days. Together they experience sex constantly—taboo sex, sordid, dirty, obscene, violent sex—no questions asked. Sex is all that matters.

Brando said the idea was intriguing. Bertolucci told him what he really wanted him to agree to was to improvise on the material. "All my actors are coauthors of my movies," the

173

director said. Brando said he still wanted to see a script.

By the summer of 1971 Bertolucci had completed a screenplay of *Tango* with Franco Arcalli in Rome, and he sent it to Brando. Then he flew out to Los Angeles to meet with him. For the next three weeks he spent most of his time at the actor's home at the top of Mulholland Drive, having long discussions on a variety of subjects: love, sex, girls, and their experiences with Freudian analysis.

At first Brando seemed moody, shifting back and forth from emotional openness to cool detachment. By the end of the second week Bertolucci had broken down some of his defenses when he confided how he'd come up with the story of *Tango:* that it had been a secret fantasy of his to make love to an unknown woman over and over again in an isolated room and never need to know anything about her. He said he'd been influenced by Louis Ferdinand Céline, the half-crazed Parisian who believed that human beings are categorized as either voyeurs or exhibitionists. He'd also been influenced by Georges Bataille, who wrote highly charged, perverse short stories about lovers so obsessed with each other's bodies they wanted to "breathe in their farts and breathe in their comes....This is what I want *Tango* to suggest," he said.

The director said he wanted Brando to superimpose himself on the character of Paul, to confront the role completely from inside himself, inside his own guts. "I had at my disposal a great actor, with all the technical experience any director would require. But I also had a mysterious man waiting to be discovered in all the richness of his personal material."

Bit by bit, Brando began to describe his traumatic childhood in Libertyville. Bertolucci listened, fascinated. It soon became obvious that the central drama in the actor's life had been his love-hate relationship with his father.

The two men did not talk about his children. That subject was off limits. Brando was having trouble with his oldest son, Christian, then in his teens, who was drinking and taking drugs. Brando could not control him, and he was worried and anxious all the time.

That fall Brando was supposed to star in *Child's Play* in New York. He thought he had got a part in it for Wally Cox, but then Cox told him he had to audition. The movie was to be directed by Sidney Lumet, but after many disagreements, Brando was fired.

In the meantime Alberto Grimaldi became the producer of *Last Tango,* even though he was suing Brando for $700,000 for his "inappropriate behavior" during the filming of *Burn!* Grimaldi happened to be Bertolucci's cousin, but he also liked the *Tango* script and thought Brando would be perfect for the role. He offered to drop the suit and pay Brando $250,000 plus 10 percent of the gross. Brando agreed immediately.

The use of Francis Bacon paintings in *Last Tango* was no afterthought. In October 1971, during preproduction in Paris, Bertolucci saw a major exhibit of Bacon paintings at Le Grand Palais. Two stood out for him, and they were eventually used in the title sequences and serve as a metaphor for the movie. The first is a portrait of a bearded and lecherous man on a red divan, against yellow and white walls. He is clad in a white undershirt, as Brando will be in several scenes. The second is a study for a portrait of a woman seated on a wooden chair in a white top and a brown skirt. She wears ugly wooden oxfords and cannot seem to meet our gaze. She could be Jeanne, the young girl in the movie, after she has murdered Paul, and she appears depleted and confused. At the bottom of the portrait is the shadow of a rat. The rat will turn up in Paul's apartment, and Brando will later swing a dead rat in Jeanne's face. It is the symbol of their decaying relation ship.

Bertolucci returned to the exhibit time and time again, and he took his cameraman, Vittorio Storaro, as well as his costume and set designers, who were inspired by the colors Bacon used: the reds, the yellows, the browns. When Brando arrived in Paris in late January—with his secretary, Alice Marchak, and his makeup man, Phil Rhodes—he went to the exhibit too.

"In Bacon, you see people throwing up their guts and then doing a makeup job with their own vomit," Bertolucci commented. "Marlon is like one of the figures in the Bacon painting," he went on. "Everything shows up in his face. He has the same devastated plasticity."

They both agreed on the casting of the nineteen-year-old baby-faced Maria Schneider as Jeanne. Schneider was uninhibited, voluptuous, a self-proclaimed bisexual, and the illegitimate daughter of actor Daniel Gélin, one of Brando's oldest friends. She had little acting experience but won the part over two hundred other actresses because when she was asked to take off her clothes during her screen test, she did so with supreme self-confidence. "She was a little Lolita," Bertolucci said, "only more perverse."

The first day she was introduced to Brando, he asked for her astrological sign. They were both Aries, they discovered. Then he sat with her in a café and, hoping to unsettle her, had a staring contest. "Is it difficult for you to look someone in the eye for a long time?" he demanded.

"Sometimes," she told him, staring back at him unwaveringly. He was so impressed he sent her flowers that evening, with a note scrawled in Chinese. "What do those characters mean?" she asked.

"I'm not going to tell you," he said.

From then on, he was "like Daddy," Schneider said later, especially in the scene in *Tango* when he gives her a bath and soaps her naked body as tenderly as he might have one of his own baby daughters.

It's interesting to note that while Maria Schneider had an amoral charm and was good in *Last Tango*, she was not great, but then Brando in recent years hadn't had adequate leading ladies. However, Schneider did pale beside Brando. Was it because she was so young and callow? Critic David Thomson called her "trite." He felt if Brando had had a really compelling woman to play opposite, she would have tested him. Or was it because, like Garbo, Brando simply dominates space and the viewer's eye automatically goes to him? Critic Andrew Sarris once wrote that Brando had to be the center of attention in his films, and even when he was acting with his peers, like Trevor Howard, say, or Anna Magnani, he constantly throttled them psychologically with ad-libs and constant takes so they became virtually invisible. Bertolucci says that Brando is "an angel as a man and a monster as an actor."

*

Just before shooting began, director and actor met, as they subsequently met every day, in private, often at breakfast, in Brando's rented apartment near the Arc de Triomphe. There they decided what scenes to do, how much to improvise, and why. (The infamous butter scene was thought up by Brando over café au lait.) The director kept reminding Brando he wanted him to find the character of Paul by remembering what was inside himself. The past, deadly and implacable, is the other big theme of *Tango*, he kept telling him.

This was the way Brando had imagined filmmaking could be: a total collaboration between actor and director. It would be like working with Kazan on *Streetcar* and Waterfront and *Zapata*. He could test himself in ways that many of his more recent directors had dismissed as eccentric self-indulgence. Phil Rhodes, who was always with him on the set, said he hadn't seen him so excited by a movie in years. He told Rhodes that in *Tango*, he would be allowed to take his improvisations further than he ever had before; he was willing to pull from himself his most painful memories. He felt challenged by the risks, although he did see it as a violation of his privacy.

The opening sequence of *Last Tango* takes place on the Pont de Bir-Hakeim, which Bertolucci had used in the first scene of *The Conformist*. It crosses the Seine south of the Eiffel Tower and west of the city and has two levels, with Métro trains traveling overhead from an elevated station. Our first glimpse of Brando is as he screams out, "FUCKING GOD!" against the roar of the train above him. The mad rush of those trains throughout the movie is a reminder of his frequent rushes of emotion.

Bertolucci admitted he was scared that first day, because "the scream was Marlon's idea. He started at such a violent pitch, I thought, 'I cannot work with this actor.' My fear lasted all that week. Then Marlon said he was feeling the same thing about me. From then on, everything went very well."

As usual, Brando was able to physicalize the character of Paul to a remarkable degree. Take his initial appearance in the abandoned apartment on Rue Jules Verne. Suddenly we see him emerging out of nowhere, hunched over by the radiator. He is dressed in a long brown cashmere coat, and he is hugging himself. It is as if he's possessed by some terrible, unconscious urge.

When he makes love to Jeanne for the first time, it's quick and primal; he bends over her, his coat still on; she wraps her legs around him. They come together convulsively, then break apart and fall on the floor, rolling away from each other, panting like animals.

The central scenes in the movie take place in the empty apartment, which serves as a background for all their passionate trysts. These are interspersed with glimpses of their real lives outside the apartment: Paul organizing his wife's funeral; Jeanne cavorting with her fiancé, a young film director, played by Jean-Pierre Léaud.

We see the scene of Paul's wife's suicide in her bloody hotel bathroom, juxtaposed with a scene of Paul and Jeanne in the empty apartment; he's insisting, "We're going to forget everything we know. No names, nothing. Everything outside this place is bullshit." It's his desperate attempt to stay in the "fucking present." For Paul, "hapenis" is the brutal domination and degradation of Jeanne, who is excited and intrigued. The sexuality they expressed was unprecedented in feature films at that time: frontal nudity, masturbation, and sodomy, all of which were explored by Bertolucci's "voyeuristic eye." At times Brando also seems to be acting out his own fantasies of anonymous, violent sex.

Although the movie appears to be totally improvised, there were entire scenes of written dialogue, which Brando kept forgetting. He began using cue cards hidden among the props and behind the camera. Bertolucci, like Coppola before him, tried to deal with the actor's inability to memorize. Was it dyslexia, as one of his friends surmised, or was it simply the actor's impulse to be so strongly in the moment that memorized words got in the way? Bertolucci came to the conclusion that "Marlon's forgetfulness was deliberate. He uses the sense of danger that comes from forgetting dialogue as a means of heightening his dramatic powers."

Bertolucci often seemed confused as to what *Last Tango* was actually about. Brando later said to *Rolling Stone* magazine, "Bernardo went around telling everybody the movie was about the reincarnation of my prick. Now what the fuck does that mean?"

Swedish director Ingmar Bergman thought the movie was really about two men. Maria Schneider maintained, "Bertolucci was in love with Marlon Brando, and that's what the movie was about. We were acting out Bernardo's sex problems, in effect trying to transfer them to the film." She added that she and Brando got along "because we're both bisexual." Later Brando wearily admitted to a French film magazine that yes, he'd had homosexual experiences, as most men had. "And I am not ashamed. I've never paid attention to what people said about me. Deep down, I feel ambiguous....Sex somehow lacks precision. Let's say sex is sexless."

Originally, Bertolucci planned to have his two actors make actual love on-screen. "Bernardo wanted me to fuck Maria," Brando said in an interview. "But I told him that was impossible. If that happens, our sex organs become the centerpiece of the film. He didn't agree with me."

After the film had been released, Norman Mailer wrote, "Brando's cock up Schneider's real vagina would have brought the history of cinema one huge march closer to the ultimate experience it has promised since its inception—that is, to embody life." But *Last Tango* ended up as a kind of celebrity drama, with Brando as its unwitting star, and indeed part of the film's shock value is the ultimate illusion that we are seeing a sex symbol actually Doing It.

A month into the shooting of *Last Tango,* Brando's lawyer, Norman Garey, phoned to tell him that Kashfi had spirited Christian away to Mexico, and the boy had disappeared. Brando interpreted this as a kidnapping, and he flew back to the United States immediately and hired a detective and a man from Interpol to locate his boy.

Christian was discovered in a hippie commune somewhere near Baja California. He was hiding under a pile of clothes, obviously distraught and traumatized. One of the hippies admitted to the authorities that Kashfi had promised them thirty thousand dollars to hide her son. It was part of her pathetic, drug-induced attempt to reclaim custody of Christian.

By that time Anna Kashfi had become a very sad, very

lost lady. Angry, deluded, paranoid, no longer beautiful, she suffered from epileptic fits and terrible mood swings and was a heavy drinker and pill taker. She had turned Christian's childhood into a nightmare, and Brando fought constantly to get custody, confessing to friends he was afraid that Christian was going to be "destroyed by his mother's weirdness." (Today, nearly destitute, Kashfi lives with a friend in San Diego.)

Brando appeared in court in Santa Monica with his son. He did not press kidnapping charges. Although the judge would not give him sole custody, he did agree to let him take the boy to Paris and stay with him for the next twelve months.

Meanwhile Brando was supposed to fly to New York for the premiere of *The Godfather*. Robert Evans kept trying to persuade him to appear. It was the biggest and most important opening of the year. But Brando refused. He did not want to put Christian through any more sensational publicity, since the tabloids had been covering "the kidnapping" for days.

By then, of course, *The Godfather* was on its way to being a huge hit, and Brando was acknowledged once again as the greatest actor of his generation. *Newsweek* magazine gushed, "The king has returned to his throne." There were cover stories in *Time* and Life heralding Marlon Brando's astonishing comeback.

Vincent Canby, in the *New York Times*, summed it up very nicely, calling *The Godfather* one of the most brutal and moving chronicles of American life ever designed within the limits of popular entertainment. He went on to say: "After a very long time in too many indifferent or half-realized movies...Marlon Brando has finally connected with a character and a film....His performance...is true and flamboyant and, at unexpected moments, extremely moving. This is not only because the emotions, if surcharged, are genuine and fundamental, but also because we're watching a fine actor exercise his talent for what looks like the great joy of it."

Richard Schickel noted, "His performance in *The Godfather* cannot be dismissed as merely technical acting. But it clearly derives from observation and imagination...and so represents the glorious culmination of his effort...to become the new Paul Muni, hiding behind accents and make-up."

By the time Brando returned to Paris with his son, his present wife, Tarita, had arrived from French Polynesia. She always made him feel especially secure, and she remained with him at his hotel until he completed filming. His huge success as the Godfather had energized him, and he improvised in *Tango* with even more intensity and commitment. He became totally invested in the role. "It was sometimes difficult to separate him from the character," Fernand Moskowitz, the assistant director, told Peter Manso.

This was especially true in one of the climactic scenes of the movie, when he talks about his past. The night before he filmed the scene, according to Peter Manso, Brando confided to Bertolucci that he wasn't sure whether he could dig so far down inside himself. It was just too painful.

Bertolucci told him, "Think of the nightmare about your children." This was a frightening dream he'd recounted to

Bertolucci a few days before. Brando glared at him as if he wanted to kill him, but he agreed to do the scene. Bertolucci was urging him to "act out," as Kazan had urged him to do in the past, with *Streetcar* and Waterfront.

His makeup man, Phil Rhodes, who had been with him on almost every movie he had ever done, said, "Bertolucci was pushing him, but once...you've scarred yourself over a period of time, and you know what you're doing, it's very easy to improvise." Rhodes had seen Brando use his hostility toward his father in a film only once before, when George Englund had urged him to base his portrayal of the ambassador in *The Ugly American* on Senior, and Brando agreed, even though he hated himself for doing it. It was the same with *Tango*. "He got caught up in how much he hated his father, and even though he felt invaded, he continued the performance."

We see him lying on the mattress, playing his harmonica, and Jeanne asks him, "What do you do?"

He starts out by describing his past. He's been a boxer, an actor, a conga player, a revolutionary, a resident of Tahiti, all the things Brando had been or had fantasized being. He speaks about his childhood: "My father was a drunk, tough, whore-fucker, bar-fighter supermasculine, and he was tough. My mother was very, very poetic, and also a drunk....All my memories of when I was a kid was of her being arrested, nude. We lived in this small town, a farming community....I'd come home after school....She'd be gone, in jail or something...and then I used to have to milk a cow every morning and every night, and I liked that. But I remember one time I was all dressed up to go out and take this girl to a basketball game...and my father said, 'You have to milk the cow.' I asked him 'Would you please milk it for me?' And he said, 'No. Get your ass out there.' I...was in a hurry, didn't have time to change my shoes, and I had cow shit all over my shoes...it smelled in the car....I can't remember very many things."

Months afterward, at a screening of *Tango* in New York, a friend asked him, "Marlon, why didn't you just wipe the cow shit off your shoes? You had enough time to do that."

Brando looked at him very coldly and answered, "You've never really hated, have you? When you hate like I do, you have to suffer the pain."

The last time we see Paul and Jeanne together, he is washing her in the bathtub, and she is telling him she has fallen in love with a man and it's Paul. His response is to sodomize her with the help of a stick of butter. In another scene, Paul sits with his wife's corpse, surrounded with flowers, and he sobs. Even in two hundred years, he will never be able to understand his wife's true nature: "I'll never know who you were."

This was the kind of risk-taking bravura performance Brando's talent had always promised. "It's as if we're seeing the purest kind of Method acting, a showcase of how an actor draws on his own resources of memory, anger, and anxiety to create a character," writes Foster Hirsch. "Brando didn't transform his emotional reality into a fiction. He simply revealed a dark side of himself, so the film is finally, on one level, about what it is like to be Marlon Brando." It was both a fulfillment and a culmination. Who else but Brando could have made himself look so pathetic as he dogtrots after Jeanne into the grimy tango palace and clowns and pleads, "What the hell! I'm no prize....I got a prostate as big as an Idaho potato, but I'm still a good stick man. I don't have any friends, and I suppose if I hadn't met you, I'd be ready for a hard chair and a hemorrhoid." And who else but Brando could have imagined the gesture he makes at the end of the film, right after Jeanne shoots him? He takes the chewing gum out of his mouth and sticks it to the railing of the balcony before dying.

At the wrap party, when *Tango* finished filming in April, Brando confided to Bertolucci that he would never again make a film like this one, that he didn't like acting at the best of times, but in this one he had felt violated every moment, every day. He even felt that his children were being torn away from him. Informing his agent, Robert French, that he would not be needing him anymore, he escaped to the beaches of French Polynesia with Christian and Tarita.

In the fall of 1972, *Last Tango in Paris* was screened for one night at the New York Film Festival. It created a sensation and inspired Pauline Kael to write ecstatically in *The New Yorker, Last Tango in Paris* is "the most powerfully erotic film ever made. People will be arguing about it for years." She went on to say that Brando had dug deep and fused more in a role than any other actor. He had "a direct pipeline to the mysteries of character."

Italian censors also helped the movie become an international cause célébre. Obscenity charges were filed in Bologna against Bertolucci, Brando, Schneider, and United Artists, alleging "obscene content...offensive to public decency, and characterized by exasperating pan sexualism for its own end, catering to the lowest instincts of the libido," and on and on. Not even a publicist for United Artists could have written such an enticing blurb for the film.

Brando refused to defend *Last Tango* and remained in French Polynesia, but Bertolucci appeared in court to argue for its merits, and his lawyer stated, "Marlon Brando personifies the fall of man. This is the message of *Tango*....The beast inside Marlon may be inside us too, but we are cowards and try to suffocate it."

The three Italian judges hearing the case agreed with the defense. The filmmakers were acquitted.

By the start of 1973 *Last Tango* was released in theaters in Italy and elsewhere. Its notoriety helped its box-office appeal, and by the time the film opened in New York in February, it had more than one hundred thousand dollars in advance sales. The Kael review (which Brando thought was vastly exaggerated), plus fulsome cover stories in both *Time* and *Newsweek*, prompted negative reviews from other critics, who called the movie "a piece of talented debauchery. It makes you want to vomit." One joked, "It gives butter a bad name." *Last Tango* went on to become the biggest moneymaker in the history of United Artists, and Brando became a rich man all over again.

The movie had opened smack in the middle of the so-called sexual revolution. Feminism was blossoming; the gay rights movement was on the rise; there were nude encounter groups and sex clubs and open marriages. *Last Tango* followed on the heels of such other controversial films as *Carnal Knowledge, Midnight Cowboy,* and *A Clockwork Orange. Last Tango* seemed to glorify the idea that sex can be impersonal; sex is no longer sacred or even dangerous. Many feminists loathed the movie and thought it was chauvinistic. But critic Molly Haskell pointed out that "in surrendering her body without strings, Maria Schneider had a better chance of ultimately freeing her mind. Schneider's journey into her entrails, under Brando's instruction, is terrifying. But if she survives, she has a better chance of possessing her life than ever before."

Brando refused most requests for interviews. He would do no real publicity for the movie; he wanted to remain in Polynesia, and he returned to Los Angeles in mid-February only because Wally Cox died suddenly, and he flew back for the memorial. But he refused to join the mourners in the Cox living room. He remained in the bedroom and listened to the speeches from there. That night he slept in Wally's pajamas.

Afterward he and Pat Cox fought over Wally's ashes. At one point the two grappled with the container, but Brando was stronger, and he wrestled it away. He kept the ashes in his car for a while, and then in his bedroom, and he told people he talked to the ashes.

He was angry at Wally for dying. "He was as close to me as my sisters are." Wally had been the one person he trusted, the one person he confided in. Oh, yes, they had had their differences. Once Brando hadn't spoken to him for three years because Cox had been unable to come to Dodie's funeral, but Wally forgave him his anger.

Not long after the memorial Pat Cox sued Brando for Wally's ashes, but within a couple of months she dropped the litigation. "Marlon needed the ashes more than I did," she said. They are now buried somewhere on Brando's property. He and Pat Cox do not speak.

*

On March 23, 1973, Brando refused to accept the Oscar for *The Godfather*, and he didn't appear at the ceremony in the Dorothy Chandler Pavilion. He sent Princess Sacheen Littlefeather to explain to the audience his position, which was that he could not accept the award after the way the film industry had treated the Indians. She was allowed only two minutes on camera, so backstage she read Brando's eloquent fifteen-page speech in full to a huge crowd of reporters. "For two hundred years, we have lied to them, cheated them out of their lands,...turned them into beggars."

Out front the audience was booing, and there were catcalls. Clint Eastwood joked, "Maybe we should give an Oscar to all the cowboys shot in John Ford movies."

At home Brando monitored the awards on three TV sets in his living room. His two sons, Miko and Christian, sprawled on the floor beside him. He was angered by the academy's reaction to his speech, but he was pleased that the two billion people around the world who were watching the awards would be aware of the brutal history of the American Indian genocide. He had accomplished what he set out to do.

As somebody who was at the ceremonies said, "It was a showstopper. The Hollywood establishment thought he was gonna come back to the fold and be a good boy. Instead Marlon really shook everybody up. Up until then it had been a very boring evening."

Marlon Brando has always had a sense of the theatrical.

16

AFTER HE TURNED DOWN THE Oscar for *The Godfather* in 1973, Brando stayed away from making movies for three years, dedicating most of his energies to the American Indian Movement (AIM), which he helped found. He was present when participants in the violence at Wounded Knee were brought to trial, and he joined the Menominee uprising in Gresham, Wisconsin, dodging bullets and trying to negotiate a truce with the National Guard.

It was his most radical involvement and also the most disillusioning for him. Some Indians were cynical about Brando's motives, calling him nothing but a publicity-seeking actor. There were rumors that at Gresham some tribe members (copying the famous *Godfather* sequence) placed a bloody horse's head in Brando's sleeping bag. There were reports that he broke down and sobbed.

Even so, he subsequently paid the bail for various AIM leaders when they got in trouble with the law. He even helped a couple of them avoid arrest and housed several top AIM leaders, including Russell Means, in his home in Beverly Hills.

For a while he and Means, an intimidating six-foot Sioux, attempted to collaborate on innumerable screenplays about Indian genocide. Directors Gillo Pontecorvo and Martin Scorsese were in on some meetings, but nothing ever came of the project.

By 1975 Brando had agreed to star in *The Missouri Breaks,* a western written by Tom McGuane. He was to be paid $1.25 million plus a percentage for five weeks' work. This was to be the actor's pattern over the next twenty-five years: to make a great deal of money in as short a period of time and with the least effort possible, so he could continue financing AIM and his various Tetiaroa projects (including one to fund a scientific study to raise cold-water Maine lobsters in his lagoon).

There were big problems with the script. Brando would be playing a bounty hunter turned crazy murderer, hunting down a troop of horse rustlers and beguiling the hell out of them before he slaughters them one by one. He declared to director Arthur Penn, "This character has no psychological spine, so I can do anything I want—move like an eel dipped in Vaseline—I'm here—I'm there—I'm all over the place." That is why he makes his first appearance in the film hanging upside down in his saddle, dressed in white buckskin and speaking in an Irish brogue.

On location on the hot Montana plains, he spent most of his free time in his trailer talking on the phone to his Indian activist friends. He loved it when shooting was disrupted by massive thunderstorms, so he could stay inside watching the rain and studying the potential for windmill power for Tetiaroa.

He and costar Jack Nicholson improvised constantly, and director Penn allowed them to, because "You gotta watch these actors." Especially in the high camp scene played in a sloshing bathtub: The two banter back and forth, and then Brando rises from the water as voluptuous as a Rubens nude, daring Nicholson to shoot him in the back.

Throughout, Brando seems to be pushing the character to the limits of credibility, as when he wades into a river and, to the consternation of cast and crew, bites a live fish in half, then swallows it. Every time he does something extreme like this, you think, "This is ridiculous," but somehow he makes it work. By the end of the movie he speaks in a southern drawl and has turned up in a granny dress and poke bonnet.

The Missouri Breaks was a huge disappointment to the public when it was released. There had been such high expectations for Brando's performance. The *New York Times* critic Vincent Canby called it "out of control." But Richard Schickel wrote, "His crazy daring, the reckless bravura, overpowers everybody else on the screen....It's as if Brando (who used to demonstrate his contempt for the medium and only gave a small part of himself) now has decided to give it too much, to parody himself. It's not so much a performance as a finger thrust joyously upward by an actor who has survived everything, including his own self-destructive impulses."

The next movie he made, on location in the Philippines in 1976, was *Apocalypse Now*, Francis Ford Coppola's sprawling anti–Vietnam War saga inspired by Joseph Conrad's *Heart of*

Darkness. Brando would be playing the power-mad Colonel Kurtz, who sets up a mini-kingdom in the jungle and is being hunted down by the CIA.

He was very sensitive about his three-hundred-pound girth, so he played around with his visual look, shaving his head and planning to dress in black. Coppola hoped to exploit Brando's weight gain; he saw Kurtz as an overeater and very self-indulgent. Eventually a compromise was reached. A crew member recalled, "They shot the scenes in such a way that Brando appeared to be six foot five instead of five foot ten—in other words, a creature of mythic proportions."

The two men spent countless nights arguing over the script (which had no ending). Finally Brando improvised a harrowing forty-five-minute monologue for Kurtz just before he is murdered and wallows in his own blood. "I laughed, I cried, I got hysterical," Brando told someone. "I've never come so close to losing myself in a part. But Francis used only a couple of minutes of the improv."

When *Apocalypse Now* was released in 1979, it shared the best movie award at Cannes with *The Tin Drum,* but most critics found Brando's performance "pretentious." David Denby wrote, "This man has become so ponderous...he is virtually unusable." Brando didn't care. He had made more than three million dollars, and he would earn more because he had 11.3 percent of the gross.

He appeared in three other movies in the 1970s: cameos in *Superman, Roots* (a TV series in which he played George Lincoln Rockwell; he won an Emmy for his performance), and *The Formula,* in which he played an oil baron, opposite George C. Scott. In the latter, his costume included a hearing aid, which was in reality a radio transmitter that fed him his lines, replacing his usual cue cards. One of his biographers, Gary Carey, estimates that he had acted less than an hour in the four movies combined and earned more than ten million dollars.

In 1982, his trusted lawyer-manager, Norman Garey, who had structured all his great money deals, inexplicably shot himself in the head. Garey had assumed the roles of legal adviser, business manager, and confidant. Brando was devastated; he had grown to depend on Garey.

Two weeks before, Jill Banner, a small, husky-voiced actress from the Midwest who had been with Brando on and off for many years, and whom he called Weonna in his auto-biography, was killed in a freak car crash. Brando attended her funeral, which was out-of-doors, but was so undone he climbed a tree and watched the proceedings from his perch. Years before, after his successes in *The Godfather* and *Last Tango in Paris,* he and Jill had gone on a trip to the family farm in Illinois to reexamine his family roots. They fought constantly. Once Brando gave her a golden apple encrusted with diamonds and pearls; then they had a wild argument on a beach in Hawaii, and Brando tore the present from her and threw it into the ocean. "Most of the women in my life have been women of color...Latin American, Caribbean, Indian, Pakistani, Japanese, Chinese," he writes. "But [Jill] was the exception, an Irish potato, and unlike the others we had a lot in common because we grew up in the same part of the country...liked the same jokes—and fought the same way." Brando still visits her grave frequently.

In the fall of 1982, overweight and depressed, he began therapy with G. L. Harrington, a burly ex-pilot from Missouri, "a wonderful and insightful man" who was once on the teaching staff at the Menninger clinic. His office in Pacific Palisades overlooked the ocean and was a haven for artists. "In some ways he reminded me of my father," Brando writes. "He was the kind of man I thought I would never like....I [told him], 'I want to get into some of the things that happened to me in the past.'

"'Oh, we'll get to them when the time comes'...but we never did...." Instead they talked and laughed and discussed politics, electronics, geology, and botany, all subjects Brando was obsessed with. "I saw him once a week and always looked forward to it....

"Once I told Harrington, 'I think I've got a lot of rage because of my father.'...

"'Well, you're not mad now, are you?'

"'Well, not right this minute.'

"He said, 'Okay,' and that was it, but for some reason that helped disarm my anger."

Brando contends he learned more about himself from Harrington than from anybody. He sent his son Christian to him, and his sister Jocelyn, and they spent hours on the phone talking to one another about their sessions. Harrington died in 1988. (Brando dedicated his autobiography, which was published in 1994, to the therapist.)

For the rest of the 1980s Brando became more of a recluse and fortified his entire house with complicated security devices.

*

Then, in 1989, he starred in *A Dry White Season,* playing a cynical lawyer fighting apartheid in South Africa. He remained hugely fat, but his performance was crisp and specific, and he was nominated for an Academy Award. The following year he starred in *The Freshman,* a sweet little fable in which he parodies his performance as the Godfather.

Otherwise he was involved in projects on Tetiaroa, such as raising turtles and constructing a windmill, until hurricanes destroyed everything he'd built on the island, including his hotel, with an estimated loss of five million dollars. After that, he retreated to his house on Mulholland Drive. It was said he'd stay in his room for weeks at a time, reading or lolling on his king-size bed (under which he kept a loaded pistol and a twelve-gauge shotgun). He'd reconstruct the Spassky-Fischer chess matches and play them over and over on his electronic chessboard. When he did go out, he often was in disguise, once as the Invisible Man, à la Claude Rains, his entire face wrapped in white gauze.

He confided to a friend that he had spent a lifetime trying to become less crazy.

He tried to focus on his family, but there were always diversions, such as writing screenplays or discussing the possibility of playing Picasso or Marx or Al Capone. When he did relate to his kids, he related "like a patriarch," his ex-brother-in-law Dick Loving said. By now he had nine sons and daughters by various wives and girlfriends, some of whom remained with him as secretaries and assistants. All his children, some of whom were adopted, have been affected in one way or another by his celebrity, his eccentricities, and his huge self-involvement.

Brando was adamant that none of them would become actors. He railed against show business. He was glad when one of his sons, Teihotu, who lived on Tetiaroa most of the time, expressed an interest in becoming a masseur. He was proud that Petra Brando wanted to become a lawyer; he eventually sent her to law school. Another daughter, Rebecca, attended the University of Arizona.

For a while after he became famous, Brando lied about having a college degree. He always stressed the importance of education to his kids: "Learn to write so you can express yourselves. Study logic. Memorize the planets." He had tried to master all sorts of subjects: Buddhism, ecology, the history of ancient Egypt, the psychology of apes.

But he couldn't get Miko, Movita's son, even to crack a book. Miko loved Hollywood glitz. The boy became friends with the musician Quincy Jones and was hired as Michael Jackson's bodyguard. He saved the singer's life when his hair caught on fire during the filming of a Pepsi commercial, and Jackson later went to Brando for private acting lessons.

Of all his children, Christian, his eldest and his firstborn, was Brando's favorite. He was the most difficult to control, because he had such a big drug problem. He had the dark good looks of his mother and his father's mercurial ways. Christian was frightened of his father. He didn't want to disappoint him, but he could never finish school. At the age of sixty-three, Brando joined Christian (then twenty-eight) in an attempt to complete a high school equivalency course. Neither of them could stick it out.

Christian was a tree surgeon for a while and then a welder. He liked to tell the story that when he was a kid and was wading in the lagoon in Tetiaroa, a shark swam by and "Pop shouted, 'Motherfucker!' and socked the shark in the snout." He wanted to be tough like his father. Once he seduced one of Brando's women; Brando mentions it in his autobiography and says he "forgave" him. The relationship began because Brando had withheld love from this particular woman, as he often withheld love from Christian, and the two had sought comfort in each other's arms. The woman eventually returned to Brando but remained friends with Christian.

Christian didn't get along with most of his siblings; he felt closest to his half sister Cheyenne, an exquisite girl who usually lived on Tetiaroa. He also had a special affection for his half brother Bobby, who was part Chinese, had long black hair, and was an expert in kung fu. Nobody seemed to know who Bobby's mother was. Kashfi in one of her many court actions raised a question about Christian's exposure in his father's house to so many different lovers and so many different half siblings, to which Brando supposedly replied that he expected his children, "regardless of who the mother was, to play together as brothers and sisters." But Christian once said of his large, unwieldy clan, "My family is so weird and spaced out, I'd sit down at the table some nights and there would always be some new addition, and I'd say, 'Who are you?'"

Meanwhile Brando continued alternately to spoil, ignore, and bully his enormous brood. According to his makeup man, Phil Rhodes, "The older he gets, the more Marlon resembles Senior in terms of trying to control and dominate."

*

But he could not control what happened on the night of May 16, 1990. On that night, Christian Brando, age thirty-two, shot his half sister Cheyenne's lover, Dag Drollet (the son of a prominent Tahitian family), in the cramped little TV den of his father's house on Mulholland Drive.

Later Christian told police that he hadn't meant to kill Drollet, but "to scare him." He thought Drollet had been beating "my little sister, Cheyenne," so he pointed the gun at him, and the two struggled. Then the gun went off, and "I saw the life go out of him," Christian said.

Nobody else was present at the time of the shooting, although Brando came into the room moments later, followed by his third wife, Tarita, who was visiting from French Polynesia. She was in another room watching television when she heard the shot, and she ran in to see what had happened. Brando took the gun out of his son's hands, and then he phoned the police. Hours later he called William Kunstler, with whom he had worked during the civil rights movement. Kunstler and Robert Shapiro, who later defended O. J. Simpson, both became Christian Brando's attorneys.

Christian was subsequently arraigned for first-degree murder, and bail was set at ten million dollars. Brando put up his house as collateral, and within the next months he had signed a contract to write his autobiography for Random House for four million dollars.

On June 26, 1990, Cheyenne bore Drollet's son, Tuki. The baby was diagnosed as drug-addicted at birth. From then on, Cheyenne was in and out of psychiatric hospitals, attempting suicide several times.

At the trial, one of the most publicized crime cases in

the history of Los Angeles, Brando testified at some length, mostly about his shortcomings as a parent: "I think perhaps I failed as a father," and though "the tendency is always to blame the other parent, there were things that I could have done differently had I known better at the time, but I didn't."

On March 1, 1991, Christian Brando was sentenced to ten years in state prison for the shooting death of his half sister's lover. The judge imposed a penalty of six years for voluntary manslaughter and an extra four years for the use of a gun, with credit for time already served and good behavior. Christian was eligible for parole in four and a half years. Today he is free and living somewhere in the Northwest.

In 1995 Cheyenne Brando, who once described herself as "the most beautiful, the most intelligent, and the richest girl in Tahiti," hanged herself at the Brando estate in Punaauia, Tahiti. She was distraught because a court decision had again denied her custody of her four-year-old son, Tuki. Tarita, Cheyenne's mother, was awarded custody and would continue to care for the child. At the time of her death, Cheyenne, a former model, had gained so much weight that she resembled her corpulent father.

Coincidentally, Brando had just returned to the screen in a film entitled *Don Juan de Marco,* playing a benign psychiatrist treating a deluded young man (Johnny Depp) who imagines he is Don Juan. "The film has serious potential to be third rate," Janet Maslin wrote in the *Times,* "except for Brando's peculiar presence and for Depp, a brilliantly intuitive actor with strong ties to the Brando legacy." An added irony: In the last scene, set on a beautiful tropical isle, Brando dances (quite gracefully) with his wife, played by Faye Dunaway. The paradise looks a lot like Tahiti.

Brando also made a film that was released in 1996, a remake of *The Island of Dr. Moreau*, the H. G. Wells classic about a mad scientist who melds humans and animals, calls them his children, and controls them with electronically induced pain. Directed by John Frankenheimer and costarring Val Kilmer, the movie is remarkable if only to behold Brando's daring and perverse performance as the doctor. Played in total drag (white Kabuki makeup, red lipstick), it is far more extreme than the checked granny dress and poke bonnet he wore in *The Missouri Breaks*.

We first see him riding grandly through the jungle in a sedan chair, bobbing atop a land cruiser, speaking in a plummy English accent, and surveying his hairy mutants, who swarm around him. "He gives a great imitation of Queen Elizabeth," someone said.

The high point of the film is when he plays Chopin's Polonaise on the piano with a tiny Muppet-like creature whose baggy eyes and enormous nose resemble none other than Elia Kazan. The movie is an incoherent mess, but Brando eclipses everybody and everything. "It's as if in this new celebrity age of genetic engineering, Brando is deconstructing the idea of actors sitting in for the gods," wrote Jay Carr in the *Boston Globe*.

Brando's celebrity has long since detached itself from the quality that made him famous in the first place. Few people today remember what he meant to us in the vastly different culture of the 1950s. Yet he still looms large.

Perhaps the critic Molly Haskell puts it best in her seminal essays on Brando. She writes: "What is the strength of his legend? How has it stayed alive in spite of so many dubious achievements? It is written in a word. Brando. Like Garbo. He is a force of nature. An element. Not a human being....There is only one Brando. Even when the actor plays his favorite role, that of the serious, socially committed anti-star, he is still one of the five or six greatest actors the cinema has produced."

Perhaps there can be no better way to sum up Brando's effect on an audience than to tell the following anecdote. Back in the 1970s, when I was first a journalist, I did a story on the Theater of the Deaf for the *Saturday Review*. I spent several hours talking with a number of leading deaf actors about their work. A signer translated as we spoke. My last question to them was, "Who is your favorite actor?" and they all answered, fingers flying, "Marlon Brando."

"Why?" I asked.

And the signer translated, "Even though we can't hear what he's saying, we know exactly what he means."

EPILOGUE

WHEN I WAS AN actress in the 1960s, I caught my first glimpse
of the flesh-and-blood Brando, one night late at an Actors
Studio benefit held at the Waldorf-Astoria Ballroom. I was
sitting with other young members of the studio at a table in
the foyer adjacent the ballroom, handing tickets to the guests
who were streaming in.

Brando, the legendary Brando, was expected to attend. He
was one of the studio's original members, and although he
hadn't taken classes there for more than a decade, his ghost
haunted the place. Many of his colleagues were bitterly disappointed that he hadn't returned to the theater to challenge
himself with Shakespeare and Eugene O'Neill.

All at once I heard a small roar, and a pack of photographers
emerged from the street and crowded into the Waldorf foyer.
Their appearance heralded the arrival of a celebrity couple,
and sure enough, Marlon Brando and Marilyn Monroe
were suddenly smack in front of me, Monroe resplendent in
a low-cut silk gown that showed off her amazingly milky
white skin and bosom and Brando next to her in an ill-fitting
tux. His face was amazing, both noble and spoiled.

No words were exchanged between us. I was supposed to hand them their tickets, but the tickets were nowhere to be found. I absolutely froze until the benefit's coordinator hissed in exasperation, "Brando doesn't need a ticket, Patti, and neither does Marilyn Monroe. *Just tell them to go right in!*"

I could feel Brando's eyes boring into my face. My cheeks flamed. Behind him, photographers were clamoring for pictures. He and Monroe posed for a few, and then reporters started asking questions. "Hey, Marlon, are you and Marilyn—"

Something prompted me to run over and open the door for them so they could escape from the media and into the ballroom. But Brando didn't move. He continued to stare at me, and the concentration level was so high that the area around me got hot. "Thanks," he said. His voice was oddly light and surprisingly gentle. For one split second he put a hand on my shoulder, and I could feel the warmth of his palm. Then he and Marilyn Monroe disappeared.

Many years have passed since Marlon Brando touched my shoulder. I've been a writer for close to thirty; now I'm documenting his life and work. And I'm still trying to figure out why this singular artist lost his way after his two great performances as *The Godfather* and as the despairing middle-aged expatriate Paul in *Last Tango in Paris*. Foster Hirsch writes that "between them, these two films define the two poles of Brando's genius—the first is his greatest disguise performance, the second his most unsparing act of self-revelation."

Stella Adler once said, "Marlon was discovered as a personality before he discovered himself as an actor or had any sense of his own identity. After he became a huge star, he was never able to resolve his primal conflicts." Maybe his brilliance was a burden, "tempting him towards a dark psychological realm he did not dare explore." Or was it because his genius made his work too undemanding for him? Paul Newman said he was "angry at Marlon because he does everything so easily and I have to break my ass to do what he can do with his eyes closed."

For the past thirty years Brando has done little of consequence in film. That's not just a waste, that's a terrible loss, but, I hasten to add, not as far as Brando is concerned. "A movie star is nothing important," he told *Time* magazine. "Freud, Gandhi, Marx—these people are important. Movie acting is just dull, boring, childish work. Everybody acts—when we want something, when we want someone to do something; we all act all the time."

Today, at the age of seventy-six, Brando lives by himself atop Mulholland Drive. He has two new daughters by his former housekeeper, Cristina Ruiz, but they are not with him; they reside somewhere in the San Fernando Valley.

He's just signed with a new agent at ICM, but there are rumors that he's broke, that he's selling his island in French Polynesia, that he's writing a book about the South Seas.

He rarely sees anybody; occasionally he'll share Chinese takeout with Johnny Depp or he'll go to a restaurant with Larry King. His main contact with the outside world is the Internet and E-mail. He communicates with many people anonymously, sometimes correcting mistakes on the Marlon Brando Web sites, sometimes disguising his voice when he broadcasts on his ham radio; he delights in doing that. He spends much of the day on the telephone, talking to old friends for up to six hours at a stretch. These friends are the same ones he's had for fifty years, like Ellen Adler, Jay Kanter, and the Rhodeses.

He recently told one intimate, "I'm going to live to be a hundred, and then I plan to clone myself, with all of my talent but none of my neuroses." He can be hilarious, this friend says, but "Marlon has irrational blowups, too, where he'll just freeze you out. He is very paranoid, especially with the people who know so much about him. He can be incredibly cruel. He brings you into his chaos, then pushes you away. Then he feels guilty about it and he starts eating."

Periodically he'll phone Oprah Winfrey, and they'll discuss their weight gains and losses. He still has grave problems with eating. He has to padlock his refrigerator; if he doesn't, he'll eat an entire Brie cheese or gorge on gallons of ice cream. A couple of times he's hemorrhaged, his makeup man, Phil Rhodes, reports. "But Marlon always survives. He has the constitution of a horse."

Why does he eat so much? Everybody asks that question. It's an easy out to say because he's the child of alcoholics; he didn't drink, so he became a food addict instead. He maintains, "Food has always been my friend. When I wanted to feel better or had a crisis, I'd open the icebox."

Maybe he wants to disguise himself behind all that lard so the real Marlon Brando doesn't have to be seen; someone told me he hated being the body beautiful because he attracted so much attention and he didn't know how to deal with it.

Before he starts a new film, he usually goes to a fat farm. His favorite one is in the wilds of England. A former girlfriend (also obese) recalls, "We were at this spa together—in bed—

watching TV, and *Streetcar* came on. Marlon told me, 'Turn it off,' but I'd never seen it, so I said, 'Please, lemme watch.' So we did for a while, and then Marlon groaned, 'Oh, God, I was beautiful then. But I'm much nicer now.'"

Recently, just before 2000 rolled around, *Time* magazine named him the twentieth century's best actor. Throughout that year his movies—such as *On the Waterfront* and *A Streetcar Named Desire*—were on all the best movies lists, something that Brando would probably scoff about, since "best anything" awards are anathema to him. "Soon they'll be giving awards to the best plumber, the best delicatessen owner—enough already!" he'd say.

Even so, he is singled out, says Arthur Bartow, head of the Tisch School of Drama at New York University, because Brando "exemplifies the continuing vitality of the American actor." Sean Penn has been meeting with him on and off for two years about directing him in *Autumn of the Patriarch.* Johnny Depp directed him in a movie called *The Brave* that has yet to be released.

The cultural critic Camille Paglia says the younger actors want to work with him because "Brando has broken the mold for actors." It doesn't matter that his long-ago stance of rebel without a cause may have stemmed more from despair and confusion than from true rebellion. He is the one who started this line of loner heroes, followed by Paul Newman, Al Pacino, Robert De Niro, Johnny Depp, and Ed Norton. "They are the tributaries."

During the summer of 2000, Brando starred opposite Robert De Niro and Ed Norton in *The Score,* a thriller directed by

Frank Oz and shot in Canada. The movie's plot revolves around an international thief (De Niro) who's about to retire with his millions when he's persuaded by his longtime fence (Brando) and his shrewd new partner (Norton) to mastermind one last score.

Gary Foster, one of the producers, invited me to watch these three generations of actors at work. I would be the only journalist allowed on the set. There was one frustrating stipulation: I could not interview them during filming. "It would break their concentration," Foster told me. I was assured we'd talk after the picture wrapped. I was not about to hold my breath.

On June 27 I arrived in Montreal and was driven out to location, a lofty tycoon's mansion in the exclusive French section of the city. After some haggling, a unit publicist passed me onto the set itself, an ornate, vaulted living room decorated with priceless antiques and oriental rugs.

The place teemed with people of all ages—makeup men, costume fitters, assistant directors, carpenters, propmen, caterers—all murmuring into their cell phones and all determined to appear as casual as possible, although the tension was positively electric.

They were all waiting for Brando. He had not been in front of a camera for five years, and his reputation as one of the grandest, most disorderly personalities of our time had preceded him. The night before, he'd worried his producers by gorging on two enormous steaks. Someone wondered if he'd throw a tantrum, demand cue cards, or have endless discussions about the script. There was already a rumor that De Niro was siding with Brando over dialogue revisions.

Soon the set was cleared except for the three principals,

and that's when I realized that Brando was already there, lolling in an easy chair, perilously fat, heavily made up, his hair tinted a pale strawberry color. Nearby, Robert De Niro, black-bearded and glowering, paced about. Then Ed Norton shambled into view, mumbling, "I feel lucky to be on a marquee with those two guys."

For a while there was silence. The two younger actors never stopped moving, but Brando remained stationary. He appeared to be dozing. But beneath his swelling forehead, a little boy grinned. Suddenly he chuckled. He laughed. He goaded his costars into responding to him. He dared them. Finally De Niro sidled over, and they began whispering to each other.

They started to improvise about whether or not Norton should be allowed in on their scam, and then Norton burst in, charged up, infuriated. He would utter half a sentence and then flounce out. The entire scene took no more than a couple of minutes, but each time the sense of urgency seemed to rise to a different level, and Brando controlled it all the way.

"What do you think I am—crazy?" He kept repeating that line over and over, and I saw that what was so interesting and mysterious about his acting was his sense of timing; it was so full of silences. Words are hopeless, he seemed to imply; he'd rather jam a piece of toast in his mouth (as he did) or take a sip of coffee or swallow his words.

When they shot the scene, the director, Frank Oz, allowed me to sit next to him in front of the monitors so I could watch the actors up close. I was surprised by Norton's versatility. His small features were amazingly expressive: One minute he was impishly decadent, the next innocent as an angel. De Niro was simply ferocious. But it was Brando who commanded my attention. It was then that I realized that at the heart of his genius was his spontaneity. He refused to be intimidated by the camera. It didn't matter to him whether the take was usable or even consistent, but when he started to act, it was like the unleashing of an animal. His sense of play knew no boundaries.

He would munch on the toast or rustle his newspaper; each time he seemed to surprise De Niro genuinely into responding in a different way; the same was true with Ed Norton.

Twenty years ago De Niro was being touted as "the new Brando," with his tour de force performances in *Taxi Driver* and in *The Godfather Part II*, in which, paradoxically, he played the young Vito Corleone. And in *Raging Bull*, as Jake La Motta, he'd done a nightclub routine mimicking Terry Malloy in *On the Waterfront*: "I coulda been a contender. I coulda been somebody." He'd been paying tribute to Kazan and Brando and their psychologically charged realism of the 1950s, and now here they were together, in 2000, along with the youthful, jittery Ed Norton, who had created such a sensation in his first movie, *Primal Fear*, as a boy with a dual personality.

While the two actors danced around him, Brando remained impenetrable. I was reminded of what Bertolucci said: that "Marlon strangely *dominates* space. Even if he is absolutely still, say, sitting in a chair, he has already taken for himself that privileged space. And his attitude towards life is different from other people because of that fact."

It was a reminder that Brando had reached another level of iconography, that the force of his personality and his reliance on behavior to illuminate character have changed the way we judge acting as an art.

SOURCES

I was first asked to write about Marlon Brando in 1977, not long after I left acting and became a journalist, but instead I chose to write a life of Montgomery Clift, Brando's principal rival in film. As a result, I began documenting the world of theater and film from the 1950s on, and I interviewed many of the men who directed both Clift and Brando—Elia Kazan, Fred Zinnemann, Joseph Mankiewicz, John Huston, and Edward Dmytryk—and I also spoke with Bobby Lewis and Harold Clurman, who taught both actors.

There are twelve biographies of Brando. I drew from the following: Charles Higham, *Brando: The Unauthorized Biography* (New American Library, 1987); Bob Thomas, *Brando: Portrait of a Rebel* (Random House, 1973); and Richard Schickel, *Brando: A Life in Our Times* (Atheneum, 1991), which not only contains the most astute analysis of Brando's films but also elucidates his special place in American cinema. Schickel's earlier book *Intimate Strangers: The Culture of Celebrity* (Doubleday, 1985) clarifies the terrible price of fame. I found critic Molly Haskell's splendid essays on Brando in the *Village*

Voice ("A Myth Steps Down from a Soapbox"), published during the 1970s, to be trenchant and gracefully written.

Also, Anna Kashfi's memoir about her marriage to and divorce from Brando, entitled *Brando for Breakfast* (Crown Publishers, 1979), the harrowing account of a couple who never should have married, is surprisingly insightful.

The most monumental biography of Brando is Peter Manso's 1,118-page *Brando: The Biography* (Hyperion, 1994). Manso spent seven years researching and writing and interviewing something like a thousand people. The book contains a wealth of information vividly documenting Brando's childhood, his young adulthood in New York, his experiences in the Broadway theater, and the behind-the-scenes stories of the making of his movies. I drew liberally from the book, and I thank him for giving me permission to do so. However, Manso speculates a lot, especially about Brando's private life and about the circumstances surrounding the shooting of Dag Drollet. I chose not to deal with these subjects in detail since the focus of my book is on Brando's work.

In 1991 Brando decided to write his autobiography, *Songs My Mother Taught Me* (Alfred A. Knopf, 1994), which he wrote with Robert Lindsey. His book came out simultaneously with Manso's, and the two books were often reviewed together. Purportedly when Brando read Manso's book, he roared, "This guy wants to be me! Why would anyone want to be me?"

As much as possible, I checked the biographers' material against Brando's own autobiography. It is an often contradictory portrait of a great artist and a superb director's surrogate who will not admit even to being a *good* actor (he claims he has no idea what his remarkable performance in *Last Tango* is about). He seems to want to be thought of as an operator, a prankster, a liar, and a con man. He has wonderful stuff in the book about his experiences in the civil rights movement; his years in French Polynesia; his feelings about nature and animals; his reaction to celebrity and money; and his devotion to the people most important to him, such as Stella Adler and Wally Cox.

In his autobiography, Brando implies that his rabid ambition to succeed and prove his father wrong is the central drama of his life, and to have blotted out the humiliation he suffered at the hands of his brutal "Pop" is his greatest triumph. Speaking of his life, Manso paints it as a shameful disaster, but Brando in his book says it hasn't been that bad, not that bad at all.

Other books that were helpful to me:

Foster Hirsch's fine book on the Actors Studio, *A Method in Their Madness: The History of the Actors Studio* (Da Capo Press, 1984); David Garfield, *A Player's Place: The Story of the Actors Studio* (Macmillan, 1980); Foster Hirsch, *Acting Hollywood Style* (Harry N. Abrams, 1991), which made me appreciate what Brando did on film. "He uses the camera more shrewdly than any other actor," Hirsch maintains. Also illuminating: Pauline Kael, *5001 Nights at the Movies* (Holt, Rinehart, and Winston, 1984); Harold Clurman's perceptive essay on Brando in his book *All People Are Famous* (Harcourt, Brace, Jovanovich, 1974); David Thomson's study, *Last Tango in Paris* (BFI Publishing, 1998); Joan Mellon's *Big Bad Wolves: Masculinity in American Films* (Pantheon, 1977); *Kazan: The*

Master Director Discusses His Films (New Market Press, 1999); Jeff Young's in-depth interviews with Elia Kazan about Brando; *Kazan on Kazan* (Viking, 1973), Michel Ciment's interviews with Kazan on his movies and on his plays. Also, Kazan's magnificent autobiography, *A Life* (Alfred A. Knopf, 1987); Ronald Brownstein, *The Power and the Glitter: The Hollywood-Washington Connection* (Pantheon, 1990); Brooks Atkinson, *Broadway* (Macmillan, 1974); Victor Navasky, *Naming Names* (Viking, 1980), the major work on informing; and last but not least, Larry Grobel, *Conversations with Brando* (Hyperion, 1991), which began as a *Playboy* interview and grew into a book of what has to be the definitive interview with Brando.

I'm especially grateful to some of Brando's friends, colleagues, and biographers who spoke to me. There are some who wished not to be named, but to those who spoke for the record, my gratitude. Thank you to Pat Cox; Phil and Marie Rhodes; Vivian Nathan; Elia Kazan; Karl Malden; Bill Greaves; Eli Wallach; Anne Jackson; Fred Zinnemann; Eddie Dmytryk; Arthur Penn; Richard Schickel; Peter Manso; the late Mario Puzo; the late Bobby Lewis. And thanks to Robert Stewart and Sondra Lee. Special thanks to Wally Cox's biographer, Robert Pegg, who gave me unpublished information; to the actor Sidney Armus, who helped me understand what Brando's "genius" was; and to Janet Coleman, actor, director, teacher, and author of *The Compass* (Alfred A. Knopf, 1990), who enlightened me about the myriad uses of improvisation in theater and in movies. My thanks to my researchers, Shannon Brady and Tara Smith. My assistant, Sharon Nettles, deserves a special mention. She faithfully helped shape and refine the vast amount of material I'd assembled; we worked long hours together, and I'm forever grateful.

Watching Brando's movies was part of my research too. Not on the list is a funny little documentary, *Meet Marlon Brando*, which the Maysles brothers filmed in one day in 1966. It totally debunks the celebrity interview and reveals a sexy, charming, mocking Brando, sparring with several idiotic reporters as he nonchalantly promotes a movie he detests, *Morituri*. Compare this with his performance in *Last Tango in Paris*, where he indulges in the same kind of wild, free-floating humor.

Chronology of Films

1950   *The Men*

1951   *A Streetcar Named Desire*

1952   *Viva Zapata!*

1953   *Julius Caesar*

1954   *The Wild One*

1954   *On the Waterfront*

1954   *Désirée*

1955   *Guys and Dolls*

1956   *The Teahouse of the August Moon*

1957   *Sayonara*

1958   *The Young Lions*

1960   *The Fugitive Kind*

1961   *One-Eyed Jacks*

1962   *Mutiny on the Bounty*

1963   *The Ugly American*

1964   *Bedtime Story*

1965   *Morituri (The Saboteur, Code-Name Morituri)*

1966 *The Chase*

1966 *The Appaloosa*

1967 *A Countess from Hong Kong*

1967 *Reflections in a Golden Eye*

1968 *Candy*

1969 *The Night of the Following Day*

1970 *Quemada* (English title, *Burn!*)

1971 *The Nightcomers*

1972 *The Godfather*

1972 *Last Tango in Paris*

1976 *The Missouri Breaks*

1978 *Superman*

1979 *Apocalypse Now*

1980 *The Formula*

1989 *A Dry White Season*

1990 *The Freshman*

1992 *Christopher Columbus: The Discovery*

1995 *Don Juan de Marco*

1996 *The Island of Dr. Moreau*

1997 *The Brave*

1997 *Free Money*

Forthcoming

2001 *The Score*

Note: As of this writing, Francis Ford Coppola planned to rerelease *Apocalypse Now* with an added hour of footage that includes greater detail involving the Martin Sheen character as well as more footage of Marlon Brando. The new version of this movie was to be screened at the Cannes Film Festival in May 2001.

INDEX

Black Panthers, 152–4, 155, 156
Bobino (Stanley Kauffmann), 19
Bogart, Humphrey, 130
Bond, Rudy, 102
Brandeaux, Eugene, 1
Brando, Bobby, 198
Brando, Cheyenne, 198, 199, 200
Brando, Christian Devi, 131, 137, 144, 157, 175, 186, 189, 195; kidnapped by mother, 181–2; Brando's favourite child, 197–8; murder conviction, 199–200
Brando, Dodie (Dorothy, *née* Pennebaker), 1, 2, 6, 7, 10, 34, 68, 80, 124, 133, 188; theatrical career, 2–3, 6, 53; drinking, 2, 3, 7, 8, 20–1, 22–4, 52–3, 113; suggests theatrical career for Brando, 10; Brando's relationship with, 21, 24, 25, 86, 88, 89, 117, 120, 121, 123, 158; and AA, 23–4, 52–3, 68, 121; collapse and death, 112–14, 120, 123, 142
Brando, Frances, 1, 12, 14, 20, 34, 60, 81
Brando, Jocelyn, 1, 2, 3, 6, 12, 14, 20, 60, 64, 77, 129, 195
Brando, Marlon, Senior, 1, 2, 3, 6, 10, 15, 20, 24, 52–3, 64, 112, 117, 118, 124, 130; violence, 1, 2, 6, 8; Brando's relationship with, 7–8, 12, 15, 19, 52, 53, 119–20, 129, 132, 133, 135, 158, 175, 184, 195; management of Brando's money, 53, 80, 111, 119–20, 132, 144; second marriage, 131–2; Brando's resemblance to, 198
Brando, Marlon:
stutter, 3; gift for mimicry, 4, 9, 18; love of animals, 7, 35, 69, 113; relationship with father, 7–8, 12, 15, 19, 52, 53, 119–20, 129, 132, 133, 135, 158–9, 175, 184, 195; early girlfriends, 8, 14; playing drums, 7,

25–6, 39, 106, 141; education, 8, 9, 10, 11, 15, 79, 81, 197; appearance/physique, 9, 35, 43, 96, 206–7; lifestyle, 10, 39, 52, 53, 59, 62, 78; early acting, 10–11; expelled from military academy, 11–12; unfit for the Army, 13–14; relationships with women, 14, 21–2, 35–7, 83, 112; androgyny, 18; early theatrical appearances, 19, 21, 22–3; relationship with mother, 21, 24, 25, 84, 86, 88, 89, 113, 117, 120, 121, 123, 158; mumbling, 22, 29, 78, 88, 90, 96, 173; screen tests, 32, 162; friendships, 36, 62, 82; sex, 37, 107, 180–1; Zionism, 38; ambivalence about acting, 38, 107, 149, 150, 165, 186, 205; money, 53, 62, 68, 71, 80, 111, 118, 119–20, 132, 134, 137–8, 144–5, 154, 160, 162, 171, 175, 191, 193, 194; anxiety attacks, 54, 68, 81, 107; visits France and Italy, 61–2; fame, 62, 91, 128, 151, 201; paranoia, 62, 206; first film, 63; relationship with Hollywood, 64, 76, 78, 79, 138, 143; screen debut, 67; relationship with Vivien Leigh, 75–6; decision not to return to Broadway, 79; marriage to Movita Castenada, 82–3, 138; Oscars and nominations, 86, 89, 110, 116, 117, 118, 126, 143, 162, 189, 190, 196; effect of Kazan's testimony to HUAC, 88, 99, 108, 111; relationship with Norman Mailer, 92; alienation, 94; dispute with Fox over *The Egyptian*, 111–12, 113, 114; engagement to Josanne Mariani-Berenger, 112; effect of his mother's death, 113–14; singing, 115, 118; relationship with Frank Sinatra, 116; forms production company, 118–19; profile by Truman Capote,

available from
THE ORION PUBLISHING GROUP

☐ **Buddha** £6.99
KAREN ARMSTRONG
0 75381 340 8

☐ **Crazy Horse** £6.99
LARRY MCMURTRY
0 75380 961 3

☐ **Dante** £7.99
R. W. B. LEWIS
0 75381 319 X

☐ **James Joyce** £6.99
EDNA O'BRIEN
0 75381 070 0

☐ **Jane Austen** £6.99
CAROL SHIELDS
0 75381 256 8

☐ **Joan of Arc** £6.99
MARY GORDON
0 75381 420 X

☐ **Leonardo da Vinci** £6.99
SHERWIN NULAND
0 75381 269 X

☐ **Mao** £6.99
JONATHAN SPENCE
0 75381 071 9

☐ **Marlon Brando** £7.99
PATRICIA BOSWORTH
0 75381 379 3

☐ **Mine Eyes Have Seen the Glory: the Life of Rosa Parks** £6.99
DOUGLAS BRINKLEY
0 75381 287 8

☐ **Mozart** £6.99
PETER GAY
0 75381 073 5

☐ **Proust** £6.99
EDMUND WHITE
0 75380 918 4

☐ **Saint Augustine** £6.99
GARRY WILLS
0 75381 072 7

☐ **Virginia Woolf** £6.99
NIGEL NICOLSON
0 75381 147 2

All Orion/Phoenix titles are available at your local bookshop or from the following address:

Mail Order Department
Littlehampton Book Services
FREEPOST BR535
Worthing, West Sussex, BN13 3BR
telephone 01903 828503, *facsimile* 01903 828802
e-mail MailOrders@lbsltd.co.uk
(Please ensure that you include full postal address details)

Payment can be made either by credit/debit card (Visa, Mastercard, Access and Switch accepted) or by sending a £ Sterling cheque or postal order made payable to *Littlehampton Book Services*.
DO NOT SEND CASH OR CURRENCY.

Please add the following to cover postage and packing

UK and BFPO:
£1.50 for the first book, and 50p for each additional book to a maximum of £3.50

Overseas and Eire:
£2.50 for the first book plus £1.00 for the second book and 50p for each additional book ordered

---

BLOCK CAPITALS PLEASE

name of cardholder ....

address of cardholder ....

....

....

....

postcode ....

delivery address
(if different from cardholder)

....

....

....

....

postcode ....

☐ I enclose my remittance for £ ....

☐ please debit my Mastercard/Visa/Access/Switch (delete as appropriate)

card number ☐☐☐☐☐☐☐☐☐☐☐☐☐☐☐

expiry date ☐☐☐☐   Switch issue no. ☐☐

signature ....

prices and availability are subject to change without notice